HURON COUNTY L
P9-CTA-832
HURON COUNTY LIBRARY
3 6492 00414620 2

Hiker Mike's Best Hikes

The Megacity and Beyond

Mike Kirby

The BOSTON
MILLS PRESS

Copyright © 2000, Mike Kirby

Canadian Cataloguing in Publication Data
Kirby, Mike, 1945–
  Hiker Mike's best hikes : the megacity and beyond
ISBN 1-55046-289-X

1. Trails – Ontario – Toronto Region – Guidebooks.
2. Hiking – Ontario – Toronto Region – Guidebooks. I. Title

FC3097.18.K54 2000   917.13'541044   C00-930497-5
F1059.5.T683K54 2000

Published in 2000 by
Boston Mills Press
132 Main Street
Erin, Ontario
N0B 1T0
Tel 519-833-2407
Fax 519-833-2195
e-mail books@bostonmillspress.com
www.bostonmillspress.com

An affiliate of
Stoddart Publishing Co. Limited
34 Lesmill Road
Toronto, Ontario, Canada
M3B 2T6
Tel 416-445-3333
Fax 416-445-5967
e-mail gdsinc@genpub.com

Distributed in Canada by
General Distribution Services Limited
325 Humber College Boulevard
Toronto, Canada M9W 7C3
Orders 1-800-387-0141 Ontario & Quebec
Orders 1-800-387-0172 NW Ontario
  & other provinces
e-mail cservice@genpub.com

Distributed in the United States by
General Distribution Services Inc.
PMB 128, 4500 Witmer Industrial Estates
Niagara Falls, New York 14305-1386
Toll-free 1-800-805-1083
Toll-free fax 1-800-481-6207
e-mail gdsinc@genpub.com
www.genpub.com

Design by Joseph Gisini/Andrew Smith Graphics Inc.

Printed in Canada

THE CANADA COUNCIL | LE CONSEIL DES ARTS
FOR THE ARTS | DU CANADA
SINCE 1957 | DEPUIS 1957

We acknowledge for their financial support of our publishing program the Canada Council, the Ontario Arts Council, and the Government of Canada through the Book Publishing Industry Development Program (BPIDP).

For Libby, the love of my life

Dance with Mother Nature and
She'll clasp you to her more than ample bosoms.
Columbanos

For when the One Great Scorer comes
To mark against your name,
He writes — not that you won or lost —
But how you played the Game.
Grantland Rice

Yes to Everything!
Hiker Mike

JUL   5 2000

Contents

CHAPTER 5

Bruce Trail Hikes 55

CHAPTER 6

Caledon and Credit River Hikes 67

CHAPTER 7

Oak Ridges Hikes 77

CHAPTER 8

Humber River Hikes 87

CHAPTER 9

Rouge River Hikes 99

CHAPTER 10

Megacity Fringe Hikes 107

Foreword

Hiker Mike thinks he discovered the trails around Toronto, but do we have news for him. He is 1,000 years too late. Etienne Brûlé wrote of his travels on the Humber River back in 1615, and John Graves Simcoe created that famous trail from Lake Ontario to Lake Simcoe back in 1793. And those fellows were only following trails laid down centuries before by our First Nations peoples.

Within the Greater Toronto area we are blessed with one of the most diverse trail systems anywhere. With a world-renowned escarpment to our west and an expansive moraine to the north, Toronto is laced with countless river and stream valleys. In addition, we have forgotten trails, some better known as sidewalks, offering endless routes through communities rich in culture, history and architecture. Off-road, on-road — there is a trail outside everyone's door.

No one treats trails with such imagination as Hiker Mike. He believes totally in the value of walking and hiking. Best of all, he shares his experiences with everyone through maps, radio, hikes and now, this book, *Hiker Mike's Best Hikes: The Megacity and Beyond,* which includes the Secret Map of Toronto Hikes. Hiker Mike Kirby is a board member of Hike Ontario, the organization representing the interests of all pedestrian traffic on Ontario's trails. He knows that trails are not only links to places, but to nature, history and health.

This book outlines 88 distinct hike experiences within easy reach of most people in the GTA, whether by car, bicycle, TTC or Go Transit. A change in direction, weather or season creates an entirely new perspective on any of the routes.

Hiking and walking are for people of all ages. Choose a route, lace on your most comfortable footwear, and become part of Canada's fastest growing activity.

PETER HEINZ
PAST PRESIDENT, HIKE ONTARIO
MEMBER, TORONTO HEART HEALTH PARTNERSHIP

Preface

Hiking up the south Florida coast from the Bahamas in the mid-
'70s, making our way back to Canada without the airfare in our
pockets, my friend Helen and I stopped in at Miami and picked
up a drive-away car to bring back to North York for some older
vacationing snowbirds. Our first night out of Miami, we happened to stop for the night at the Dunes Motel at Vero Beach,
Florida. Every room was unique, furnished with an eclectic mix
of artifacts brought back from owner Captain Jack's expeditions
on the high seas. Moroccan tiles, Chilean tapestries, stained glass
from some Castilian cathedral, and a dining table carved out of
a single plank of Norwegian oak 4 feet wide, 40 feet long and half
a foot thick!

That morning at breakfast it was raining quite heavily, pro-
hibiting beach action or comfortable travel, so when Captain Jack
sauntered into the dining room and asked if any and all would like
to accompany him on his grand tour of the motel, most of the
patrons jumped at the idea. For the next two hours we listened
with rapt attention to Captain Jack's tall stories while he nipped
on a flask of Jack Daniels, which kept emerging from his buck-
skin coat pocket with a not-so-quiet regularity.

After lunch back at the dining room, in came Captain Jack
once more, this time quite drunk and asking if anybody wished
to accompany him on a tour around his motel, which of course,
once again, we did. This time, the Captain's stories were completely different from his morning's recollections. The Moroccan

tile was from Guatemala, the Spanish stained glass from Portugal, and the oak dining table from the Congo. When my friend Helen challenged Captain Jack on the veracity of his statements, the Captain pulled himself to his full height and said grandly, "Madam, I'd rather be a liar than a bore any day."

What has this recollection to do with Hiker Mike? Perhaps a little of Captain Jack has crept into my hiking reports. I would never lie to you outright about where I've been and what I've seen, but I just can't help myself when it comes to embellishing the truth. So keep that in mind when I speak to you about the Oak Ridges Moraine reminding me of the Himalayan Mountains, or hiking in the Palgrave Forest being equal to stepping into the Yucatan jungle. I hope there is a little Captain Jack in all of us. Don't you find, gentle hiker, that Panavision is much more exciting than small screen and Technicolour far more vivid than beige?

Hiking is my passion. When I dream of disappearing into the woods for a day-long adventure hike, I feel the same kind of rush any normal human might at the thought of a great bottle of Scotch, a nine-course gourmet dinner with friends, or an entire evening of mad, ecstatic lovemaking. You see what I mean? I turn into a horny 16-year-old at the thought of a hike. My unbridled journalistic enthusiasm for hiking may colour my reporting. You may feel that I go overboard with some of my descriptions — and you're probably right. I can't help exaggerating to make my stories appear more exotic and exciting.

Hiker Mike's Best Hikes: The Megacity and Beyond chronicles the rollicking adventures of a bunch of inveterate trespassers who hike the parks, ravines and river valleys, the Oak Ridges Moraine up Aurora way, down to the Lakeshore's Martin Goodman Trail, out to the western frontier of the Niagara Escarpment's Bruce Trail, and eastward to Port Hope and the beginning of the Ganaraska Trail.

When CFRB program director Bob Mackowycz found out about me and my hardy band of trekkers — we call ourselves the Urban Sherpas — he asked me to report live from the trail to the Weekend Morning Show with John Donabie, to share my dance with Mother Nature with the listeners. So a lot of what you'll find in the pages of this book comes from those Saturday- and

Sunday-morning Hiker Mike Reports on radio station CFRB AM 1010. Plus you're getting some visuals — such as the Secret Map of Toronto Hikes — that radio listeners don't get.

You'll notice my hikers on some of the trails. They can tell you what kind of hike to expect. Easiest are the Kids and Grandma hikes; more challenging are the Coureur de Bois hikes; experienced hikers looking for adventure will want to try the Guerrilla hikes; and the Wheelchair Babe will show you the paved paths. Many of these hikes offer you the opportunity for both easy and challenging hikes — the difference could just be which side of a river you're exploring.

I've featured hikes within an hour of Toronto. How to get there, where to park, what you'll expect to find along the trail, where to go for lunch or libation after the long trek, and how to get home, sometimes by TTC, or how to go about just camping out in a bed and breakfast for the weekend. But most of all I want to share the feelings aroused on each different adventure, more of my emotional point of view — the joy of the hike, incidents, accidents and misadventures, not just here in Megacity but every-where I hike in the world. You'll soon see how Hiker Mike com-pares the Caledon Hills and the south-facing slope of the Oak Ridges Moraine leading down to Lake Ontario to the foothills of the Himalayan Mountains in Nepal.

You'll know I'm only exaggerating, right? I'm only kidding! The Himalaya are much bigger, but the pine forests and river valleys and spectacular vistas of the Moraine really do remind me of the Khumbu region on the trail to Everest.

Adventures on the Comeback Trail

How It All Began

I'd been sober for three months in September '85, on my 40th birthday, and I was casting about in quiet desperation, looking for a project to take my total concentration and energy, and keep me out of the saloon. I got the call from my agent that my services were needed for a big play at Theatre Calgary called "K-2, The Mountain Show." The story concerned two climbers trapped on a snow ledge at 27,000 feet just under the summit of the world's second-highest and most dangerous mountain, K-2, in the Karakoram Range of the Himalaya. When I discovered that the show was a two-hander to co-star my dear friend and great actor John Evans, I accepted immediately, little knowing that this play would put me on the trail that would change my life forever.

Research would take me to the Rocky Mountain foothills of Kananaskis Country, where I was taught to climb rockface, and to the Banff Museum to learn about life survival in the high Himalaya. The librarian handed me a Japanese photographer's

collection of portraits of the great mountains of the world, and upon opening the gargantuan coffee-table tome, I gasped out loud at what I saw. Everest, Lhotse, Ama Dablam and K-2 were more monstrous and megalithic in scale and size than anything I had hitherto witnessed on Earth. I couldn't believe my eyes. I vowed to see for myself when the play was finished.

And so it came to pass that in the spring of '86, I booked passage on an Air India flight to New Delhi, and on to Katmandu in the Himalayan Kingdom of Nepal.

There I was to meet with my now-lifelong friend Joe Pilaar of Canadian Himalayan Expeditions Trekking Company, who was to guide me up through the Khumbu Region along the Dud Kosi River, past Namche Bazaar, Tangboche, and countless Sherpa villages to the great frozen lake at Gorak Shep and the Everest Base Camp at just under 20,000 feet, where the climbing expeditions

begin their assault of the highest peak of the Earth Mother, Chomo Lungma.

I was 40 years old and in pretty good running shape, but that only put me in the ballpark. The trek was far more difficult than I ever imagined. Because we had flown into the Hilary Airport at Lukla, already at 7,000 feet, I had not properly acclimatized my body to that ever-increasing lack of oxygen, and so for the next nine days of my journey, moving upward into the rarified air, I became sicker and sicker. My head pounded during the midday climb because my sunglasses did not keep out the ultraviolet rays. My heart and lungs worked overtime to keep my aching legs moving up the trail. I couldn't really appreciate the spectacle of the Buddhist monks clad in their saffron robes, and their sky temples, or the ever-happy, shining-eyed Sherpa tribesmen we encountered on the trail.

Closing in on the Base Camp, one breathless step at a time, I suffered an extreme anxiety attack. But, after having convinced myself I couldn't go home without satisfying the mandate, I stood at last on the peak of Kalapataar at 18,500 feet, smiled at my success, and then puked out what little I had left in my stomach. And while doing my rendition of the rainbow flash, I looked down on the Base Camp while surrounded on all sides by a ring of the highest mountains in the world. Lhotse, Everest, Nuptse, Ama Dablam, Tam Serku, an entire 360-degree eye-popping vista. I could die now. The rest of my life would be downhill from here.

Although I had lost 16 pounds somewhere on that endlessly upward trail, I'll never forget that special superhuman feeling I experienced descending into the rich oxygen on my homeward journey. I felt stronger with every downward step. Arriving back in Katmandu at 2,500 feet, my senses so finely tuned from my journey to the sky, the colours, sounds, sights and smells of the ancient caravan city shot through me like electricity. And after 23 days of rigorous abstinence I was so horny I could have shagged the crack of dawn. Instead, we clean-living and well-married men proceeded to eat everything in sight during what little time we had left in that magical mountain kingdom of Nepal.

I had finally learned from hiking what running couldn't teach me. With proper preparation, I could walk anywhere in the world for an entire day, enjoy a great meal and a good sleep, and without any stiffness or body pain, I could rise the next morning and hike the same distance, once again, for the whole damn day. And again. And again.

At 40 years of age — kind of my halfway point, I'd like to think — this daily hiking regimen agreed so completely with how I wanted to live the rest of my life. Walk 5 to 6 miles every day, the same distance I used to run, only now I take twice as long to do it, and have twice as much fun, and enough time to think things through in order to solve any current problems, thereby blowing out any stress. And so I came back from the Himalaya with a completely new lifestyle, which, over these past years, I have had little trouble carrying through. It's so simple. I always make time for a two-hour hike every day, and if work or family keeps me from the trail and my muscles start to twitch and my attitude gets downright gnarly, I'll go out  after dark when the kids are asleep and do the 6 miles out and back to Vicky Keith Point Lighthouse on the Leslie Street Spit on Toronto's eastern waterfront, just so I can get to sleep.

(Hikers: Thank you in advance for your patience when I stray off the metric path. That 6 miles is, in fact, almost the same as 10 kilometres, but my German-made car and Canadian-made brain still judge distance Imperially. Most trails around here are measured in kilometres, but you'll discover I use both metric and Imperial. I promise I'll steer clear of hectares, rods and hands.)

Hiking is in my blood, and I'll do it till I drop. Six-time Olympic medalist, gymnast Leon Stukelj has a little advice for us in his 100th year here on Earth: "It's not a secret at all," he says. It's ingenious. "Don't smoke. Drink a little. *Walk a lot.* And don't haste for life." This is a man who, when presented with his 100th-birthday cake, grabbed hold of the arms of the chair in which he was sitting, hoisted his frame into the air and kicked his legs straight out while supporting himself with his arms. Live, love, laugh and be happy, hikers. A wonderful place from which to begin.

Don't you think?

HUG THE RUG

Most of us sit in a chair to read or watch TV, slouching slovenly in a quasi-fetal position with our knees somewhere up around our double chins. Get out of your chair, hikers, bend over and hug the rug. Nuzzle your nose into the nap, face down, spread your arms and legs and give your rug a great big hug. It's great for the joints this time of year. We use our bodies more in summer with swimming and baseball, but we veg out and stiffen up in the dark and dreary winter months. So here's what you do, hikers.... You gotta stay loose. Create your own intimate relationship with the floor. Spend your leisure hours doing some stretching exercises, relaxing your poor, fat, tense, overwrought body. How about a couple of push-ups or sit-ups — just a couple — we don't want to make it unpleasant, right?

"Great," you say. "Sure I'll try that floor exercise and relaxation stuff, Hiker Mike, but just one question. How the heck do I get down there?" Well, I'm glad you asked. You just squat down on your haunches and then roll onto your back. Then when you want to get up, climb onto your hands and knees into the squat position and let your ever-strengthening legs take you up. Squatting keeps you loose in every joint — your ankles, your knees and your hips — and what's best of all, squatting aligns your spine. We've all seen aboriginal people in those *National Geographic* documentaries squatting in front of their huts or around the fire, even the grandmas and grandpas — it's one of primitive man's naturally assumed positions.

Let's get right down there and reintroduce ourselves to the floor. Take a pillow and a book with you and spend some quality time. You'll like the floor and the floor will shine right back at you. Hang out on the floor for the winter and it will keep you loose as a goose in your old age. Besides, how can you fall down and break your hip when you're already down there? Let's get old and healthy and happy together.

CHAPTER
2

Inner-City Hikes

TAKE A HIKE.

WEIGHT LOSS!
-o-
CELEBRITIES!
-o-
& L.S.D.*

* LONG, SLOW DISTANCE

In the mid-1600s, Samuel de Champlain dispatched his staunch lieutenant Etienne Brûlé to Upper Canada to explore the northern coast of Lake Ontario, all the while searching for a trade route to Hudson Bay and points north and west. Anchoring at the mouth of the Humber River, Brûlé must have been astounded. "The land between the rivers," as early Toronto was known to the aboriginals, was protected on all sides by weather-moderating natural land-masses: to the west, the giant limestone cliffs of the Niagara Escarpment, cutting off wind and snow from the Great Lakes; to the north, the Halton and Caledon Hills and the mighty Oak Ridges Moraine, those great huge humps and bumps of sand and gravel under which many rivers find their source before rushing headlong down our southern slopes to Lake Ontario. Those rivers — the Credit, Humber, Don, and Rouge — and the creeks — Etobicoke, Mimico and Duffins — all contribute to the wonderfully diverse ecosystem of the Megacity, rewarding us with an incredible variety of waterfront, river and mountain hiking trails.

Along the northern coast of Lake Ontario, the waterfront trails include the Martin Goodman Trail, running through downtown Toronto from Oshawa to Burlington, and the three-hour Toronto Islands hike from Wards through Algonquin, Centre and Olympic Islands to Hanlan's Point and back. Add to these a spectacular array of inner-city forays through Toronto's countless multicultural neighbourhoods, ravines and industrial parks, and you have set the table for a substantial hiking smorgasbord. I have been reporting on hiking trails in the Megacity area twice a week for over two years on radio station CFRB, and the following are the absolute best I can recommend to you.

The Runner and the Big Biscuit

Back in the late evening of the Age of Aquarius, a group of us, inner-city show-biz types, decided that we would have to do something about our declining physical prowess. After all, we were in our early 30s, and the generous amount of abuse we were heaping upon ourselves must sooner or later be balanced with some kind of rigorous exercise, or we would surely be dead by age 50.

The 10K long slow distance craze was sweeping the city. Parks and ravines were rife with runners all colour-coordinated in the latest Brooks and New Balance marathon styles. It got so bad you couldn't step into a green space for a toke without being run down by the Central YMCA 10K club. Running was the sport of choice in Toronto, and what better place? The forest city boasts more vernal escape space than Banff, Alberta.

We lived in a big old farmhouse next to the Waterworks in the Republic of Rathnelly, and just down the street, across Poplar Plains Road, began Winston Churchill Park — a mile-long, shady green hollow, tracking under Spadina, all the way up to Loblaws at Bathurst and St. Clair. Every morning the Hangover Running Club — Hiker Mike, artist Dan LeBlanc, actors Barbara Williams and Shawn Lawrence, and little brother T. Daniel Kirby, attorney at law — would set forth on a 10K grand circuit adventure we jokingly called the Big Biscuit. This monster inner-city route took us up through Winston Churchill across St. Clair, north across Heath Street and up through Cedarvale Ravine to the Eglinton West Subway stop. We would cross at the light and run up the east side of the Allen Expressway to the Beltline, an old abandoned railway that once delivered wood and coal fuel to North Toronto citizens from the Dominion Coal Yards at Merton and Mt. Pleasant a hundred years ago.

The old Beltline Trail, now a natural cinder running path, bisects the backyards of the Forest Hill and Chaplin Crescent rich and famous, and flies over Yonge Street at the TTC Yards at Davisville, and into the Mount Pleasant Cemetery across Moore

Park and southward into the Rosedale Ravine, up past Milkman's Lane into the Balfour Park, to Summerhill, across Yonge and westward home to Rathnelly. Total time: one hour, give or take, depending on the hangover.

This antidote to our abuse lasted until 1986 when, after finally sobering up for good, I realized that although the LSD (that's "Long Slow Distance," not the hallucinogen) had been keeping my heart and liver alive, the running had also been taking a heavy toll on my ankles, knees, hips and back, and now that I was 40, something was going to give, big time!

Fortuna has always been my friend. She raises me up most times, and she has dashed me down others, but I believe, as have most Medieval and Renaissance men, that one must be ready when Lady Fortuna offers you the opportunity of a lifetime. And so it was that after doing the play "K-2, The Mountain Show," and continuing on to hike the Himalaya the following spring, Fortuna brought me at last to walking the world. So from then on, with the possible exception of moving quickly at times to dodge downtown traffic, I was never to run again. The hike's the thing. And now we walk the Big Biscuit, or a similar inner-city hike, for two hours every day. Here are some of my favourite inner-city hikes that I'm sure you'll enjoy as much as I do.

2. Summerhill Nature Trail

So, you feel like you should be going on a hike but you really don't have enough energy to do a big one. Well, have I got a hike for you! Get off the subway at the Summerhill Station and walk down to the end of Shaftesbury Avenue, and you'll see a little sign that says Nature Trail. The pathway takes you right into the Rosedale Ravine, one of the prettiest ravines in all of Toronto. It's like hiking 200 years into the past. Fifty-six steps take you right down into David Balfour Park. Use the little bridge to cross the creek and turn right, southbound. Cross Mt. Pleasant — busy traffic but it's worth it. The path takes you through the Park Drive

Reservation along a babbling brook straight down into the Don Valley. It's quite peaceful and there's a green canopy of leaves over the road in summer, making it very quiet. Follow this beautiful cinder road past the floodgates and the sign to Milkman's Lane. This whole area is designated for unleashed dogs: this is where my Malamute, Rupert, comes for the Big Sniff.

You'll find the whole Don Valley stretching out in front of you. Follow the path north past the Old Toronto Brick Factory, the Heath Street Pedestrian Bridge, and voila! There you are at Moore Avenue. Cross the street into Mount Pleasant Cemetery, and the path leads you back to Yonge and the Davisville TTC at Merton. The whole trek is two hours to the Davisville Station. Be sure to stop in at the Second Cup and have a nice cold watermelon drink before you hop on the subway. You'll be home in a Megacity minute!

HIKE TO WORK

Canadian winter's a pretty dark time of year. It's easy to worry and brood about the credit cards and bills over the holiday season, so lighten up. By taking a hike we get a chance to work out our problems and think things through with no distractions. A good two-hour hike brings about relaxation and a feeling of well being. If you hike after dinner for an hour or so, you'll lighten up around the waistline too.

Let's get out of our fat pants. How about setting a realistic goal of half an inch a month off the waistline? Two hours a day will do it.

Hikers, our winters are becoming mild enough to seriously consider walking or biking to work every day. Think of how slim and healthy we'd become if we were to boot it to work five days a week, then go for a hike or two on the weekend for recreation. I admire and I emulate people who hike to work and home each day. Take, for example, our executive producer at Sound Source Networks, Jean Marie Heimrath, who bikes to work every day from way out in the 'burbs. He's a lean, mean fighting machine. We could tear a page from his daytimer.

Now's the time to up the exercise ante, hikers. We're going to be living a whole lot longer than our parents and grandparents, so we may as well enjoy being 85 and healthy. And if we're good-looking — bonus!

The Old Indian Escarpment at Yonge and St. Clair

I've made a wonderful discovery outside the doors of CFRB at 2 St. Clair Avenue West. The big hill upon which St. Clair is built is called the Old Indian Escarpment and it runs west for miles from Yonge Street through some of the most wonderfully rich neighbourhoods in Toronto. And the views from the top of the Indian Escarpment range all the way south to the Toronto Islands and the blue Lake Ontario horizon beyond. We normally don't see these views because they're restricted to the backyards of the old money perched on the edge of the Escarpment, but I'm going to show you how to access the view.

From the St. Clair Subway, walk south on Yonge Street to Farnham Avenue West, to Avenue Road, where you'll find the De La Salle Oaklands Private School. The hundred-year-old yellow-brick edifice is complete with gothic turret from days gone by. Cross Avenue Road at the stoplight and head west on Edmond Avenue to Poplar Plains and into the Clarendon Estates. These are the mansions with the million-dollar view. The old money, movers and shakers of Muddy York, the Vaughans and the Straughans and the Jarvises, once lived here, a couple of hundred years ago. Some of the Eatons still do, but where, I'm not telling!

This morning, the sun was streaming from across the lake through the backyards. When I stopped my daydreaming and resumed my inner-city boot, Clarendon spilled me out across Russell Hill Road and into Winston Churchill Park and then onto Spadina Road south to beautiful Casa Loma. As I saw her, crested on the Escarpment, the city behind her shining in the morning sun, I revelled in the old dowager's majesty. Benevolently smiling down on her subjects, she rivals any Florentine villa, French chateau, or castle on the Rhine in my book.

Enough musing! Now it's time to descend the 109 Casa Loma steps of the old Indian Escarpment along Spadina Road past the busy Davenport, just a few short blocks to the Dupont Subway, and you're already homeward.

Inner-City Hikes

The hike is only an hour. Stop at the Indian Rice Factory on Dupont at Howland Avenue for lunch. Hiker Mike's favourite? Chicken curry on rice and a big Coke.

4 Sherwood Park

What was Little John's name before Robin Hood changed it? John Little. And where did that hardy band of outlaws live? Sherwood Forest of course, east of Mt. Pleasant, south of Lawrence right here in Megacity. And that's where we're hiking today, a 10,000-year-old glacier valley, and this ecological niche is what Toronto looked like up to 1750 — all bush — deciduous and Carolinian forest mix right here in the centre of Toronto. Watch out for falling coconuts, hikers, and the Sheriff of Nottingham.

Family hikers with dogs and kids walk the trail east to Bayview and back. One hour! A great hike for seniors. And for you coureurs du bois, cross Bayview and follow the creek east to Sunnybrook Park. Heavy going creekside — mudslide and thick underbrush — so no sneakers, please. Walk Sunnybrook past the horse stables and up the hill to the end of the road and voila! — the Tom Thomson Trail. Make the big circle on the horse trail around the playing fields to the south and west and back you go to Sherwood Park. Two hours of golden groove.

And thanks to Tracker Dave, singer-songwriter David Bradstreet, for taking me. We had a ball. Adults don't go out in the forest for adventure any more. We've got to get back to the garden and play like when we were 12-year-old kids. Hiking our parks and trails stirs our youthful imaginations, and improves our youthful, rugged good looks. As Robin Hood himself once decreed, "Rise up from thy expanding posterior, Bumholio, and take a hike through Sherwood Forest, for the sake of thine own health."

5 Discovery Walks

L et me extol the virtues of the Toronto Region Conservation Authority. Allow me to sing the praises of the countless parks, ravines and river valley trails of the Greater Toronto area: Albion Hills, Glen Haffy, Glen Major, Palgrave Forest, the Rouge, the Humber, Scarborough Bluffs and Highland Creek, to name but a few. A hiker's haven, every one. And so it is with great pleasure I can announce that the inner-city arm of Toronto Parks and Recreation has put together six — count 'em, hikers — six new Discovery Walks right here in the middle of the city. And every Discovery Walk is tucked into its own colourful and informative brochure with directions on how to get there, what to look for on the trail, a history of the trail's origin, and a step-by-step map of the trail.

The Discovery Walks are a series of self-guided hikes across the length and breadth of our Toronto.

1. The Garrison Creek Ravine from Christie Pitts to Fort York
2. The Central Ravines, Beltline and Gardens, through Mount Pleasant Cemetery and Moore Park
3. The Eastern Ravines and Beaches, through Glen Ames Creek and Glen Stewart
4. The Western Ravines and Beaches, including High Park and Grenadier Pond
5. The Don Valley Hills and Dales
6. The Northern Ravines and Gardens, through Alexander Muir Park and Sherwood Park

And these Discovery Walks are designed to show how the parks, ravines, gardens and beaches link all the neighbourhoods in our city. These walks are not on the Secret Map, but the Discovery Walks brochures are yours, free for the asking: phone my pals at Parks and Recreation Community Services Division at 416-392-1111 or pick them up at your local library. Now you can start your own inner-city hike at your closest TTC stop.

HIKE YOUR WAY TO SKINNY

Ron Brown's a personal trainer from Kitchener, Ontario, and he says in his book *The Body Fat Guide* that you can burn off fat by hiking for two or three hours every weekend. This translates into an inch off the belt-line every month, so we can be skinny and beautiful in time to pig out during the Christmas party season. There are a whole whack of Boomers out there who don't want to play tennis anymore and the old 10K/marathon runner has damaged the hips, back, knees and ankles so badly that running has become painful. So why not slow down and enjoy the exercise? Hikers take twice as long to do it and have twice as much fun. Take a friend along and talk up a storm, or just listen to your Walkman. Hiking isn't rocket science, folks. Just one foot in front of the other for two to three hours every weekend and talk to me in a year. I guarantee you'll be stronger, skinnier, sexier and full of the joy of life.

6 High Park

Yesterday morning right after the report, two-time Genie Award-winning actress Linda Sorensen and I drove out to the west end of Toronto with every intention of walking the Sunnyside boardwalk from the Humber Bridge to Ontario Place and back, but the Gardiner was closed and the Lakeshore was jammed and we couldn't turn left against the eastbound traffic to get to the beach. Then Fortuna smiled and delivered us into High Park at the Colborne Lodge Drive.

It had just been a month since we'd been here for the Hike Ontario Day festivities when the Urban Sherpas led a hike through High Park, but I really wanted to go back and explore the park off the beaten path. So, starting at the bottom of the park, we found a series of bush and creekside trails that wound their way east and north around the outside of the park all the way up to Bloor from the Lakeshore. We put together an easy one-hour hike through the High Park Zoo down behind Colborne Lodge, up the Spring Creek Nature Trail, past the greenhouses, the "Dream in High Park" Amphitheatre, around the vegetable garden plots, down to the woodchip trail alongside Spring Creek, again up past the pines from east to west across the top of High Park, through the Sports Complex, and down the west side through the oak savannah to Grenadier Pond, and up to Howard's Tomb right next to Colborne Lodge. A big, fat counter-clockwise circle. Total time: 1½ hours. A great inner-city hike for beginners, seniors and kids.

Taylor Creek

Come back with me now to yesteryear, to 1831, when Captain Phillip DeGrassi, veteran of the Napoleonic Wars, exercises his right to a 200-acre grant and purchases the Don Valley. Move on to 1927, as erstwhile Boy Scout and camper Charles Sauriol realizes his lifelong dream and buys the East Don Valley, donating it back to the City of Toronto. And now, we own it — it's ours, folks. The whole darn Don Valley! And the Charles Sauriol Conservation Reserve just happens to be at its centre, and emanating from it, a half dozen of the best hikes in Toronto.

Taylor Creek Park Hike is only 8 kilometres roundtrip — about 90 minutes. Imagine the greenest of river valleys surrounded by emerald hills and trees, and right down the middle, running on either side of the cascading rapids, are two trails, one for bikers and one for hikers. Oh, holy day! There are fitness stops along the way where you can do torso twists and toe touches. Why, you can even jump a log if you've a mind to it!

Taylor Creek Park's not too difficult to find: Take the Danforth Subway to Victoria Park and walk north to Taylor Creek Park, or drive to Don Mills Road north of the DVP and pull in at the big Sauriol Park sign. Come on, all you ex-runners, ex-tennis players, and hit the Comeback Trail with Hiker Mike. Hikers take twice as long to do it, but boy, are we ever in "kinda sorta shape."

Warden Woods

I call this hike Serendipity in Scarborough. Hiding at the south-west corner of Warden and St. Clair lies a wonderful hike into the Warden Woods, a trail that eventually joins with Taylor Creek Park, spilling you out into the Don Valley and the world beyond.

As you descend into the pretty river valley you're surrounded by traffic on two sides and the TTC subway line on the third. You're not 50 steps into the valley when it soon becomes very quiet with the sounds of nature. River rapids and waterfalls and birdcalls reign supreme between the deep dark green walls of the river valley, keeping the sounds of civilization at bay. Along the paved riverside path, you can see the backyards of some very lucky landowners high up the banks of Massey Creek, while you find yourself surrounded by evergreens and sumacs, newly planted to anchor the riverbed for future floods.

This hike to the south and west, which will deliver you into the Pharmacy Avenue Metro Works, is a most civilized, cultivated trail, and accessible for kids, grandpas and wheelchairs — lightly graded, easy and paved. The whole valley's a peaceful sun-pocket sheltered from bad weather, and if you take kids with you, you'll have a heck of a time keeping them interested in the hike, because they'll want to play in the river shallows or climb the trees.

The Massey Creek eventually joins the Taylor Creek. Heading west, you'll have to cross Pharmacy and Victoria Park very carefully as there are no crosswalks, but you'll soon find yourself in Taylor Creek Park leading you into the Don Valley Sauriol area, so you can literally walk to work downtown from Warden and St. Clair to Bay and King. It'll take you three hours, but just imagine foregoing the subway once a week. The famous singer Salome Bey has been known to walk two hours a day and has finally lost a whole other person, more than 100 pounds. So step off the treadmill of life, hikers, and dive into the tranquillity of Warden Woods. Park for free in the TTC lot on the northeast corner of Warden and St. Clair.

9 East Point Park, Highland Creek

And now for you adventurous inner-city hikers, the folks at Metro Conservation have opened up the path from Lake Ontario at East Point Park, all the way up the Highland Creek to Colonel Danforth Park on Old Kingston Road and the Military Trail. This is a wonderful two-hour roundtrip hike. East Point Park lies at the bottom of Beach Grove Drive south of Lawrence Avenue East in the Morningside Meadowvale area. You can even take the bus there. Call the TTC for info (416-393-4636); ask for Betty and tell her Hiker Mike says hi.

10 TTC Camping The Indian Line Campground

Hikers, you know I like to harp on about how fortunate we are to live in such a diverse biosphere in the greater Toronto Area. And once the good weather is here, our Canadian instinct stirs us to take to the countryside and revel in the greenery. But what if you're newly married and flat broke with no car? How you gonna get outta town? What if you're new to Toronto, from Calgary, say, or Kosovo, and you don't know your way around? Or what if you're young lovers whose parents will not allow you to sleep together under their roof, and you just can't find any privacy? What are you poor people to do? Wanna go camping?

Did you know that there are two huge Metro Conservation Camping areas within our Megacity? Mind you, the Albion Hills Campground is way the hell up Highway 50 north of Bolton and a little tough to get to, but the Indian Line Campground lives at the corner of Finch at 27, and here's the grabber that puts it in reach of every guy and gal. You can take the TTC to the Indian Line Campground. That's right, bunky, jump on the bus with your lady fair and head first to the Canadian Tire where you'll outfit yourselves with a tent, an extra-large sleeping bag and a flashlight. Then back on the bus to the Indian Line Campground. Once your tent is squared and pegged, you can have a shower, do your laundry and get a Coke and a Mars Bar at the tuck shop, then bus it over to the mall for dinner and a movie. Then back to the tent for a night of raucous passion in the forest primeval.

In-town camping is an exceedingly inexpensive getaway from the everyday, courtesy of the Conservation Authority, the TTC, and Hiker Mike, who thought it up. All you newlyweds, newcomers and immigrants to our fair city, rise up off your booming economy backsides and go TTC camping right here in our Toronto.

Hiker Mike's Wish List
The Bayview Path

You know that we have a wonderful hiking and biking trail running all the way from Yonge and Bloor down the greenery scenery of Rosedale Valley Road to Bayview, but once you hit Bayview, hikers are SOL, if you know what I mean, because there is no hiking path running north-south on Bayview. Hikers T-bone with a dead-end fence.

The Martin Goodman Trail is on the far east side of the Don River, and because of the fence, it's impossible for hikers to get there even if they want to swim. On the way home the other day I noticed there were 50, maybe 60 people walking up the soft shoulder on Bayview with their books, backpacks and briefcases coming home from work and school. So isn't there something we could do? There's a nice green space between Bayview Avenue and the river, just perfect for a path, or how about a nice storybook bridge over the Don to the Goodman Trail, where we could walk our way north through the Chester Springs Marsh, or down to the Lakeshore and out to the beaches. So please help us out with a little pathway where Rosedale Valley Road meets Bayview Avenue, Mayor Mel. Councillor Ila Bossons. How about it, guys?

Now speaking of Metro Councillor Ila Bossons, this wonderful lady and neighbour in our Summerhill Gardens has initiated a spring cleanup the first Saturday of May. All the neighbours grab a big garbage bag and head to the nearest ravine or park and pick up all the garbage that has gathered over the winter. We inner-city hikers can do much the same in our own neighbourhoods, either organizing a work party with our friends or simply taking an hour out of our lives and filling up our own little garbage bag. Last Saturday I wandered over to the Little Park in Summerhill and tried to make up for my dog Rupert's unauthorized dumps over the winter by picking up between 5 to 10 pounds of everybody's dog poop. It's the little things, hikers, that make us feel part of the community. Besides, just the simple act of bending over will do wonders for our backsides. And speaking of which, now's the time to get up off that big fat thang and hit the trail. Give that trail a good whack for me, will ya?

THE SECRET MAP OF TORONTO HIKES

Before we leave the back porch today here at Hiker Haven, let's talk maps. Maps are the fantasy lifeblood of hikers. Just looking at a map gets me so excited, I gotta hit a trail. Lisa Rotenberg and I have designed a Megacity map for you, with all the greenbelt and river valley hikes from Oakville to Pickering and beyond. It's like looking at our city from high up in a satellite. This is the perfect map for you family hikers and coureurs de bois and you'll find it in this book. It's like you're flying over Toronto from Brampton and Mississauga in the west to Scarborough and the Bluffers Park in the east, and with all the river valleys in between. The two that excite my imagination are the Etobicoke Creek and the Mimico Creek, side by each, running from Confederation Park down to Lake Ontario. When you're ready to move further afield of Toronto and graduate to guerrilla tactics, head on down to Mountain Equipment Co-op on King between Spadina and Bathurst, and pick up the topographical maps of the Megacity area, containing all the hills and river valleys in our area. Now you're cooking! Make up your own adventure.

CHAPTER
3

Inner-City
Waterfront Hikes

The Mystery of Sadavis: Sharon Davis e-mailed me again. She was mad as hell that I called her S. A. Davis on the Hiker Mike Report. I thought she might have been a guy, an Eastern Indian gentleman named Sadavis — S A Davis — get it?

She writes, "I decided to hike from my home in East York and take the Martin Goodman Trail along the Lake Ontario waterfront to High Park, then Parkside Drive up to my office. Things I learned on my hike: 1. I love walking in the rain. 2. There are almost no cyclists on the Martin Goodman Trail when it rains. 3. The eastern section of the Martin Goodman Trail passes through some of the ugliest urban/industrial areas imaginable."

Then Sharon goes on to suggest that I wrap up my show with these words, "So hikers, if you want a vision of a post-apocalyptic Toronto, and you don't mind horrible, nose-burning smells, or a noise level that would drown out even the most tormented wails, I recommend a brisk stroll through the ravaged landscape that makes up much of Toronto's central and eastern waterfront." Miss Sadavis, I beg to differ. The industrial lakeshore area is the last frontier for industrial Megacity hiking — Cherry Beach, Unwin Street, Regatta Road, Leslie Spit. It's God's country, Sharon, because most sensible Toronto people are still too scared to go there. The only thing that stinks in the Eastern Beaches is that damned sewage smokestack, and it'll be gone soon. And if we get the 2008 Olympics, the whole Parliament-to-Leslie corridor will be totally transformed into the Olympic Village and gone forever, so now's the time to explore. And when you're finished hiking, head up to Queen Street east of Woodbine and hit the Second Cup and the bagel joint next door for lunch, Sharon. Just make sure you check the wind direction before you go, and if it's blowing from the east, blowing the sewage into your face, skip the hike altogether and go directly to the Beaches for bagels and coffee! But keep those e-mails coming, Sharon, you're my breath of fresh air.

The CNE to the Humber Bridge

This hike, a late-summer hike, is dedicated to the Grand Old Lady of the Lakeshore — the Canadian National Exhibition. Let's use this hike as a warm-up to the Ex. We all know how to get to the Ex.

Take the Queen Streetcar to the Dufferin Gates and walk south through the Arch past the Bandshell and take the bridge across the Lakeshore. Yikes! We're on the Martin Goodman Waterfront Trail. Follow the trail west, towards our destination for today — the bridge across the Humber River.

First up is the Argonaut Rowing Club on the water, and Marilyn Bell Park, where she came ashore in '54.

Next, the Boulevard Club. But members only, hikers. No sneaking in and playing with the lawn-bowling balls. When you come to the old Palais Royale, turn left and walk down to the Boardwalk right on the water straight out to Sunnyside Pool and Beach, where you can swim and sun and have lunch or just pause for an ice cream at Breyers. Why, you can even rent a canoe for an hour! Now it's only 15 more minutes to the Humber Bridge and boy, is it spectacular! It opened in '94 and looks like a huge balloon bicycle tire rolling through the Humber. The hike is only two hours roundtrip from the Dufferin Gates, so pack your bathing suit and a couple of bucks for lunch and make it a day at the beach. And pick up a little litter if you see any to keep our Megacity clean and shiny.

Toronto Island Hikes

Every half hour or so on the weekend, the Wards Island Ferry leaves the bottom of Queen's Quay, and 10 minutes later, after a wonderful weather-filled ride, you tumble onto Wards Island and the best waterfront hike in Toronto. Head south across the baseball field past the cottages till you hit the boardwalk, turn west and don't stop until you come to Hanlan's Point next to the Island Airport, an hour later. Anytime is a great time of year to see the Islands, 'cause once you leave Wards for Centre Island, you are absolutely alone, three seasons of the year. The Yacht Club, the amusement parks, the playgrounds and the beaches are all empty

— just you and Mother Nature. Once you get past the breakwater, head down to the water's edge and walk along the beach, all the way to the airport. Roundtrip is two hours. Stop at the Rectory Restaurant for lunch on your way back to Wards Island Ferry. Great hike for kids with the added bonus of a ferry ride.

In winter, those poor island ferries at the foot of Bay Street have to break through the ice each time they make the crossing. Normally the fireboat comes through every morning at five o'clock and makes a path through the ice, but not so in the Blizzard of '99. If it gets much colder they'll shut down the ferries for good until the spring, then the island folks will have to take the airport ferry way over at Hanlan's to get home.

Crossing from the mainland towards Wards Island, you get the panorama view. From the southeast to the west, the cottages of Wards Island and Algonquin are easily visible through the barren trees, then on to the RCYC and the abandoned amusement parks of Centre Island and in the far west, Hanlan's Point and the airport tucked up under the CN Tower and the Skydome. We only had two hours to spend on the Islands because of the winter ferry schedule, so we decided to hike the 3 miles from Wards to Hanlan's Point and back.

The Toronto Islands are a picture-perfect postcard right out of New England, peaceful, quiet and serene — I'm moving there!

PATH OF LEAST RESISTANCE

Hiking is Mother Nature's path of least resistance. It's good for stress and worry. Got a big exam coming up? Or a big meeting? Take a hike for an hour or two with no distractions. The blood pumping through your brain will bring your thoughts into focus. If I've got a problem to solve I hit the trail and work it out.

I finally found out how to lose that extra tire I've been carrying around my middle. Every night after dinner, during that TV and reading time I once used for chips, cookies and popcorn, I now go for a two-hour hike before bed. When I come home I have an orange or a bowl of cereal before turning in and I can easily lose 5 to 10 pounds a month. Try taking a break halfway through your hike for some O.J. and a chocolate bar. Bring along an extra pair of warm, dry socks to change into at the halfway mark. Your feet will thank you. By the way, Hiker Mike wears SmartWool socks.

Snow piled up high and white, the wharves and docks all ice-glazed and deserted. But the road on the Toronto Islands was perfectly shovelled for the two cars, the van and 50 pushcarts that use that road. This blizzardy weather doesn't bother the islanders — they're a hearty breed. Riding a 40-mile-an-hour sou'wester at our backs from Hanlan's to Wards, we hit a terrible whiteout; the Centre Island Pier vanished, along with our road, but we found our way back just in time for the return ferry ride to the mainland. Bashing our way through huge chunks of ice, we made it back to the mainland docks and our snow-covered cars, parked next to Captain John's Restaurant, and were home in front of a fire in less than half an hour.

If you've got a great sense of adventure, hikers — go where they're not — the midwinter Toronto Islands hike is just what the fat doctor ordered. It was the great Greek scientist Archimedes who said, "Mother Nature will give up her secrets to you, if you just love her enough," and it was Hiker Mike who said, "Up, hikers, up off those ever-expanding backsides and take a deep winter hike to the Toronto Islands."

Regatta Road
Outer Harbour Marina

If you're looking for a great inner-city hike full of good weather, or bad for that matter, take Cherry Street south of the Lakeshore, past the rock 'n' rolling Docks Nightclub, turn left on Unwin Street, and right on Regatta Road. You can park in the Sailing and Surfboarding lot and hike along the water east towards the Beaches on the Martin Goodman Trail, with sailboats on the right and the Hearn Generating Station on the left. It gets a little gay down there, hikers, so, like they say in Tangiers, stay on the main trail.

When you come to the rickety one-lane bridge, cross it, then turn right into the Outer Harbour Marina, where the real adventure begins. This hike is a cross between the New Jersey Meadowlands and the Out Islands of the Bahamas. Low-slung berms of land jutting out towards the Leslie Street Spit create a great hurricane hole for sailors to lay up during bad weather. If there's any pure weather to be had in Toronto, hikers, it's here. Last winter Captain Karl and I got caught in a freak blizzard whiteout with high winds when, moments before, there were blazing blue skies. When you come to the security gate tell them you're going in to see your friend Mitch Gold on the good ship *Halcyon,* Slip 94, then skirt the marina, stay on the road and hike to land's end.

There you'll find a ship's bulkhead in dry dock. Climb up into the wheelhouse and experience a view of the Toronto skyline all stately and majestic that'll steal your heart away. This hike is flat and mostly paved so even your grandmother can do this hike, so take her along!

There must have been some vandalism or theft recently, because security has been beefed up at the main gates of the Outer Harbour Marina. My daughter Maryanne and I went for a hike out there Christmas Day '99, and we were turned back. So we just cut across the field past the offices and hiked the Leslie Street Spit instead. Give it a try.

Inner-City Waterfront Hikes

P.S. For all you young and beautiful grandmas out there who are insulted and offended because you think I'm talking about you, I'm not. I'm talking about *your* grandmas, so stop picking on me. Your true friend, H.M.

Leslie Street Spit
Tommy Thompson Park

If I could keep this hike a secret and not have to tell anybody about Tommy Thompson Park or the Leslie Street Spit, I would. I've never felt so much a part of nature while hiking in the city. And I am totally blown out by this juxtaposition of nature and the city. I find myself walking along the Spit's quiet country road, out into Lake Ontario, with bush and lagoons all around me, and through a break in the trees I see the Royal Bank building, the CN Tower and the Skydome — the whole damned beautiful travel poster of downtown Toronto. And so many millions of birds out here, I feel like Tippi Hedren in that Hitchcock picture. I've been out this way

WILE E. COYOTE

We were out on the Leslie Street Spit on a cold, clear star-lit night, knee-deep snowdrifts on the road, and just as we came upon the channel bridge at the halfway point to the lighthouse, we were hit with the shrieking howl of an aggressive, protective coyote. The sound shot an arrow of primal fear through our hearts. Tracker Dave gasped audibly, Hiker Mike froze in his tracks, and Rupert the Malamute climbed into the warm spot between my legs. This was definitely a Keep Out warning, and it sure worked, because immediately we reversed our course and headed back. We'd gone far enough for one night.

This was truly a profound moment; when the call of the wild shouted out to the people of the city to go no further across the channel bridge and please, for once in our lives, leave the wildlife in peace.

during nesting season and the terns have indeed severely harassed Rupert and me with bloodcurdling screams and poop bombs.

The 3-mile road to the lighthouse and Vicky Keith Point is paved, so wear your cushy shoes! On the overhead light-standards sit the biggest, fattest seagulls you've ever seen. Go around! Way around! Tommy Thompson was the Metro Parks Commissioner who is responsible for all the parks and ravines in Toronto, and he's also the man who invented the saying "Please walk on the grass." And out on the Spit he gives you almost 500 acres to do it.

You know what we have here, folks — our own Cape Cod, complete with lighthouse, marine life, boats and skyline. The Leslie Street Spit is just like being 3 miles out on the ocean with no city sound. But because of all this peace and serenity, I have difficulty maintaining my pace. I keep slowing down! So this may be just what the stress doctor ordered for us city folks: 3 miles to the lighthouse and 3 miles back equal 2 hours. Tommy Thompson Park is my number-one hike. Take the Queen Streetcar to Leslie and go south, hikers!

The Beaches Boardwalk to Glen Manor

'Twas a damp, cold and gloomy Sunday morning with a bitter northwest wind screaming down the Lakeshore at the Beaches when Tracker Dave Bradstreet and I went to meet the Beachman at Ashbridges Bay. The plan was to leave one car there, then drive back across the city to begin the 12-mile hike from East Humber Park at Kipling, along the Martin Goodman Waterfront Trail back to Ashbridges. It's a great hike past the Ex, Ontario Place, and Harbourfront, but this time Mother Nature slammed the door. The trail was impassable. We couldn't even find it for the snow. The Goodman Trail was as icy as Sister Mary's glare! So we Urban Sherpas put our heads together and this is what we came up with. We hiked the mile or so of the Beaches Boardwalk east, with the wind at our back, past the Olympic Pool and Kew Gardens until we came to that Palace of Purity — the Harris Waterworks — at Victoria Park and Queen, then we doubled back along the Boardwalk to Glen Manor Road north across Queen Street, then up the Glen Stewart Ravine and Ames Creek, one of the few remaining natural streams in Toronto.

All of a sudden we found ourselves on one of the Toronto Parks and Rec Discovery Walks. Four-thousand-year-old artifacts have been uncovered along the Ames Creek. So keep your eyes open. You could find a frozen hairy mammoth or a million-year-old Beaches man buried in the muddy Ames creekbed. This hike will take you north through the neighbourhoods of the late-1800's small lakeside resort (known then as the Beach) up Glen Manor Road to the Kingston Road TTC and back down to the Beaches Boardwalk by way of Balsam Avenue and cobblestoned Pine Crescent. A cornucopia of architectural beach-manor splendour. Two hours tops. Stop at the Second Cup or Licks on Queen Street just east of Woodbine before heading home.

17 Scarborough Bluffs

Hundreds of feet above Lake Ontario, high atop the Scarborough Bluffs, stands a string of emerald green and snow white parks, watched over by my favourite folks at Metro Conservation. And the jewel in the crown is the Rosetta McClain Garden, maintained in perpetuity as a "quiet and restful detour on the busy road of life."

Hike the Bluffs east along the ridge and neighbourhood streets, from Kingston Road and Birchmount to the bottom of Brimley and the Bluffers Park. The two-hour hike is mostly flat except for the extremely steep down and up to the Yacht Basin, but along the way you'll be witness to the most fantastic vista views from the top of the Bluffs. Far below, you see the rock jetties fingering out into the lake, moderating the current and preventing further erosion along the shore. And rising up from the waters below, giant mud mesas carved into eerie shapes by wind and weather. (One of them, Macho Point, has a razor-thin path tightroping its way out into nothingness, with sky on all sides.) Down in the Yacht Basin, you high-enders can lunch at the Dogfish Restaurant while the rest of us coureurs de bois grab a Coke and a smoke, squatting and looking out to sea, hopelessly lost in a dreamy reverie, before heading back to our cars at Birchmount.

Don't miss this one, hikers. Scarborough Bluffs is a gas, gas, gas. Any questions?

NIGHT HIKING

Can you feel it? Springtime? This is the time of year when the sap starts to run and we feel the springtime energy pulse through our veins. We've got to take advantage and ride this energy wave back to fitness by doubling up on our hiking time.

We've got a rowdy little group called the Urban Sherpas that get together every night at 9 pm at various hiking venues around the Toronto area: usually well-lit footpaths such as the Rosedale Valley, the Cedarvale Beltline, or Cherry Beach, the Beaches Boardwalk or Sunnyside. Good and safe. Lots of hikers, bikers and Sherpas on the Comeback Trail. We always get in about an hour-and-a-half walk and we're back home in bed just in time for Lloyd and, boy, do we sleep. And I'm so refreshed when I get up. Go grab your best pal, hit the trail, and we'll all look like a million bucks this summer in our skin-tight bathing suits. Hike every night for an hour and "You're beauuuutiful, baybay."

Don River Hikes

Time
flies like an
arrow →
BUT
Fruit flies
like a banana.
— HIKER MIKE —

Pottery Road to Riverdale Zoo

I'm sitting in the Don River rapids just south of Pottery Road wetly reporting "live" to John Donabie on the CFRB weekend morning show while Rupert the Malamute wrestles with a salmon who would rather just lay her eggs and be gone. There is no more beautiful hike any time of year than our own Don Valley, but before we start our trek from Pottery Road to the Riverdale Zoo, it's time for Backpack Trivia. So I reach into my backpack and out comes this question. Which army captain returned from the Napoleonic Wars a hero, and was granted hundreds of acres of the Don Valley as his prize in the early 1800s? They also named a TV series and a street in Toronto after him. Who was he? Captain Philip DeGrassi, that's who! You'd know if you'd been paying attention. Are you being have?

Getting there: Start your hike at the Broadview Subway just north of the Danforth. Walk two lights north, turn left on Pottery Road and go down into the Don Valley past Todmorden Mills and Fantasy Farm. (What in heck goes on in Fantasy Farms, anyway?) At the bridge to the Don River, take the Martin Goodman Trail to the left and hike south past the rapids and Chester Springs Marsh, to the Riverdale Bridge and up into the zoo you go! Say hi to Bert and Barney Burrow, and the chickens and the cows, and take a beverage at the English Tea Garden at the corner of Sumach Street and Winchester. Walk out to Parliament Street and catch a bus home. Total time, two hours.

R-E-S-P-E-C-T!

While hiking, remember to take only photos and leave only footprints. Protect your wilderness — there will never be more of it.

19 Pottery Road: West Side of the Don

You know how excited I get when I discover a new 1,000-year-old trail? I'm doing the neutron dance. What's so beautiful about this Don River Trail is that it's so close to home and it's right across the river from a path I've walked a hundred times. I reported to you from the Pottery Road Fish Hatchery last fall when Rupert tried to take that salmon for a hike. That's the well-used Martin Goodman Trail running up the east side of the Don. Well, forget about that side of the river, hikers: too many bikes this time of year. Cross over the river. It's the west side we want to be hiking. At the corner of the Bayview Extension and Pottery Road you'll find Murphy the flower guy, and if you ask Murph where the west side path is, running north, he'll point you the way. He'll even let you park and he'll watch your car, if you buy some flowers from him when you get back. Remember, the path you want runs right next to the rail tracks on the west side closer to Bayview. Head north.

It's a walk on the wild side, hikers. Big willows hang out over the river with ropes for swinging — the kind of path you find when you are 12 years old, on your bike with your buddies, and you're looking for adventure.

Follow the west side path up the Don to the Sauriol Reserve and walk the easier Martin Goodman Trail back south. The west side of the Don is an in-town Himalayan foothills adventure and cardiovascular contest, ups and downs for days — a very old, hard clay path 4 to 6 feet wide that'll have your heart and lungs screaming for mercy. Mountain bikers have always used this trail, from kids on Schwinn balloon-tire bikes, to ultra-sophisto mountain and trail bikes today. So share this five-star trail with the bikers, hikers, — they're friendly enough. It's so worthwhile.

Just one whiff word of danger, hikers. Do not try this trail when it's raining. The clay turns as slick as WKRP's Herb Tarlek when it's wet. They'll carry you out in pieces. Remember. The west side is the wild side. You're looking at two hours minimum.

20 South Sauriol to Sunnybrook Park

I've got a "go where they ain't" hike for you, you know, like hiking ski trails in the summer and the waterfront pathways in the winter. Quick, before the bikers take over one of the nicest two-hour trails in Toronto, find your way to Don Mills Road north of the DVP and a big sign saying Sauriol Reserve and Taylor Creek Park.

Once inside, follow the signs for Sunnybrook and hike the 5K north along the river through the Seaton Park and the great stone gates of Sunnybrook, past the Police Stables where Megacity's finest keep their horses. The Metro Parks guys have set up some bleachers by the horse pasture so you can have your lunch and appreciate the horseflesh. Then head up the big hill to the end of the parking lot east of the Sunnybrook playing fields. There you'll find another Tom Thomson Trail through the high hardwoods down into the Seaton by way of Wilket Creek and Sauriol, and the big circle takes you back to your car — two hours tops.

21 Tom Thomson Trail

Tom Thomson Trail is an inner-city hike buried behind a parking lot in the very back of Sunnybrook Park. You'd never find the trail in 14,000 years. That's the time it took to form the glacial ridge along which it runs, high above the Wilket Creek. You see, hikers, this is my neighbourhood. I've walked south from Edwards Gardens along the Wilket Creek down to Pottery Road, in the Don River Valley, countless times, looking up at that dark and mysterious wall of a thousand greens, wondering quietly to myself if there was anything in the way of trail up there. And now we know! Thomas H. Thomson was so enamoured of Sunnybrook and Mother Nature, his friends and family had the trail built for, and dedicated to, Tom. (Not to be confused with Metro

Parks guy Tommy "Please walk on the grass" Thompson with a P.)

As you leave the back Sunnybrook parking lot, the high hardwood forest welcomes you into a long and dark green tunnel spilling you out onto the high north-south ridge overlooking the Wilket Creek. Through the trees far below, you can see the Edwards Gardens Trail running creekside south on its journey to the Seaton and Sauriol Parks, further down the Don Valley. If you stay up on the ridge, the Thomson Trail will eventually spill you out onto the horse trail across the playing fields, the restaurant and the Sunnybrook Stables, and back to your car. The hike is so rugged, so civilized, so neighbourly, so...so Toronto.

Speaking of neighbours, next time you're talking to that snoopy busybody who lives across the street from you, tell him to take a hike, and show him your boots. If he doesn't take it the wrong way and try to get you arrested for assault, maybe he'd consider going for a hike with you. He'd probably make a great hiking buddy and quite possibly end up being a fellow inveterate trespasser. So put your local nosy parker to work discovering new trails in your neighbourhood and beyond. Hiking's a great way to get to know somebody. People open up on the trail, share their hopes and dreams with you, and their sandwich if you're lucky.

We've added a new hiking club section to the Hiker Mike website (hikermike.com) with all the names and phone numbers of the hiking clubs near you, so you now can join in and take a different hike every weekend. You'll find that list in the back of this book on page 168.

Sunnybrook Park to Edwards Gardens

Here's a Do-It-Yourself Megacity Hike from Peter Heinz, past president of Hike Ontario. Park the car in Sunnybrook Park just north of Eglinton Avenue on Leslie Street opposite the old Inn on the Park. Hike north. Follow the signs to Wilket Creek Park and visit Edwards Gardens, and as you head back south, turn right when you cross the little bridge and climb the hill. Now you can roam the vast expanse of Sunnybrook Park past the Police Stables. Follow the river back to your car. You've just seen nature at its best and you've never left the city.

On your way back, cross the suspension bridge into Serena Gundy Park and climb the horse trail to the top of Toronto's Matterhorn — a high, rugged pinnacle jutting up through old-growth white pines. A heart-pounding hike up its steep flank affords you a full 360-degrees view of the entire Don Valley. The horse trail by the bridge is marked with orange-painted posts and black-and-white woodcarvings of horse and rider. Serena Gundy Park feels a lot like Stanley Park in downtown Vancouver. Deep, dark and ancient.

23 Sunnybrook to the Toronto French School

After 25 years of running and walking up to Sunnybrook Park on the east side of the Don River and turning around at the stables, I finally crossed to the west side of the Don and followed my nose north along the river, leaving Sunnybrook Park far behind me. Hiking this Easter Monday afternoon, there were hordes of hikers and bikers and moms and dads pushing buggies, but once I crossed the river, all the people disappeared.

The west side of the Don is an environmental floodplain with lots of newly planted trees and no city sound. The pathway spills you into the Glendon College Campus. Keep close to the river. On the far side of campus you'll cross a hundred-year-old cement bridge, turn right and cut under the Bayview Avenue Bridge. Look up and you'll see the beautiful new Cheltenham condominium at Lawrence and Bayview. Look down and you'll see a beaver dam right under Bayview Avenue! A lot of trees have been chewed up for beaver food and housing. We've got rich people in the Cheltenham, we've got salmon in the Sauriol, and beavers in the Don! God must be in heaven because all's well in the Megacity.

Once under the Bayview Bridge you bump up against a golf course, with fences that not only block both sides of the river but the river itself. For shame! So I follow the fence up the hill and, lo and behold, I end up in the playground at the back of the Toronto French School at the corner of Lawrence Avenue and Milden Hall Road in North York.

So how's this for a great idea? Take the TTC to the Toronto French School and hike down the Don River through Sunnybrook, down the Don Valley on the Martin Goodman Trail, to the Lakeshore and out to the Beaches for lunch. That's a good three-hour hike, and think of how hungry you'll be! Take the TTC home! I'm forever seeing side trails that beckon me to follow, and this time I'm so glad I did. Now I've added a new section to the West Don north of Sunnybrook, even though that big bad golf course has stopped us from continuing our quest for the source of the Don, which lies to the north in the Oak Ridges Moraine. Perhaps through the good work of Hike Ontario president David Francis and Metro Conservation, who have authority over all river valleys in Toronto, we will one day see pedestrian walkways beside every river, from the top of Toronto to the Lake of Ontario. 'Tis a consummation devoutly to be wished!

HIKER MIKE LIFESTYLE DIET

Hiker Mike has big appetites. My life has been a series of adventures just trying to deal with them. It took me years to shake off a strong penchant for Jack Daniels, but shake it I did, and now I even say no to hard drugs. There's so much else we can enjoy in life, like great food. So through my own experiences, both good and bad, I've finally come up with a Hiker Mike Lifestyle Diet. And here it is! Hikers, you can eat absolutely everything you want, within reason, of course. Meat, fish, fruits and veggies, peanut butter and jam, ice cream, New York cheesecake — if — you walk two hours a day. It's not that much to ask, is it? Walk to work and home again. With this kind of exercise you can eat anything you want, but no piggy behaviour. Two hours of hiking or exercise a day gives you the right to eat with impunity, so go ahead, hikers, you're entitled, and while you're at it, please pass the cheesecake.

Salmon in the Sauriol

CFRB News honcho Taylor "Hap" Parnaby mentioned in the news yesterday that the salmon have come back to the Don River as far north as Lawrence Avenue in the Sauriol Reserve. Hikers, this is the first time since 1874 that we've had salmon that far up the Don, so three cheers to Metro Conservation Authority for leading the attack on cleaning up the Don Valley.

I was standing on the Eglinton Bridge overlooking the Don River valley just last week and, as I glanced north up the river into the Sauriol Reservation, I noticed there was no riverside path. That was good enough for me. I jumped over the side into the valley below and found a level of high ground running between the river on my left and the railroad tracks on my right. And so began my journey up river to the top of the Sauriol, trailblazing as I went for the first kilometre or so. What I've found works best for me is to keep to the river when in doubt. The animals have to drink, even in town, so what you'll find at the river's edge are a series of walkable animal trails that intersect every which way, but are totally navigable for hikers with little feet — the exception is Florida's Everglades, where alligators make their trails from river to hideout. And sure enough, as soon as I passed under the railroad bridge, there it was in all its glory — the wide and gentle Sauriol Trail running all the way north to Lawrence — a wonderful trail that rises hundreds of feet above the river with an astonishing view to the southwest and ending up in the Sauriol parking lot just southeast of Lawrence and the Don Valley Parkway. Do you know what I did next? I turned around and hiked back down to Eglinton. So now I can call the Sauriol Trail mine. *All mine.* Hurry, before a path develops. Don't hesitate, hikers! Time flies like an arrow, but fruit flies like a banana!

Top of the Sauriol

I was jammed up on the Don Valley Parkway north the other day, when I just couldn't stand it any longer and I escaped east on to Lawrence Avenue to get out of the traffic. My fairy godmother must have been watching out for me, because immediately to my right was the sign for the Charles Sauriol Conservation Reserve. I didn't realize it came up this far north. Serendipity! I wheeled in at the sign, down the hill and into a brand-new parking lot. And there I found a well-worn groovy path heading south along the east side of the Don River disappearing into the bush. And what a bush! Jungle vegetation, thick vines falling from above, berry bushes and thorns crossing the path, but I just couldn't seem to get away from the damned noise of the traffic. And just as I was thinking about turning around, the Sauriol Trail swung away from the DVP and charged headlong into the leafy quiet of the forest primeval.

Now hikers, wear your boots and long pants, because there are lots of burrs and thorny shrubs across the path, a small price to pay for such a beautiful hike. Cute little bridges cross the creek, corduroy roads span the marshes, and sandy beaches with sparkling shallows kiss up to the flanks of the Don River. I saw a big blue heron fly downriver. That's a sure sign that there is nobody around. I could be up at Glenn Haffy, it's so shady and quiet. The path climbs a hundred vertical feet up the Don Valley wall, giving you great vista from the top of the cliff and a ridge walk along the edge that will make you cry "Mama!"

This is not an easy hike. Definitely three-star, coureurs de bois. So, make it an end-to-end. Park one car at Lawrence Avenue and the Don Valley and the other at Don Mills Road and the DVP and give yourself a two-hour hiking treat.

Put your boots to it, hikers.

The Source of the East Don

I've got the gypsy in my soul. Last week I went in search of the source of the East Don River high up in the Oak Ridges Moraine, those great huge humps and bumps of sand and gravel that run across the top of Toronto — the source of the Humber, the Credit, the Rouge, the Don and the Duffins. One major street north of Major Mackenzie off Dufferin is Teston Road. Turn right and park under the Ministry of Natural Resources southern research station sign. Jump the fence and hike south on the old tractor trail that will take you into the abandoned 1940s village of Maple — old wooden buildings all boarded up. Walk through town and you'll hook up with a big, fat wood-chip pathway at the south end of town that'll take you down to a little creek. If you follow the creek, which is tough going — you'll have to do some bushwhacking here — you'll find a dammed-up lake, and bubbling up through the ground is one of the sources of the East Don River, complete with cement dam and diving platform for a wonderful refreshing swim at your turnaround point.

Next time I'll follow the source downriver in my quest to hike the East Don River in its final rush to Lake Ontario just south of Lakeshore Blvd, and the Don Valley Parkway. I figure that's a good 15-mile hike. Once I've got it all mapped out, you'll be the first to know. We'll feature the hike in Volume 2.

GO WHERE THEY'RE NOT HIKES

I'm hiking in the dead of winter on a well-used trail and there's no one in sight. You know where I am, hikers? Cherry Beach on the Lake of Ontario, and I have it all to myself. Know why? Hiker Mike's Magic Formula: Go where they're not! Go to the beach for fall, winter and spring, and in summer, hike the ski trails. You'll never see anybody! If you want a crowd, hike the Eaton Centre!

CHAPTER
5

Bruce Trail Hikes

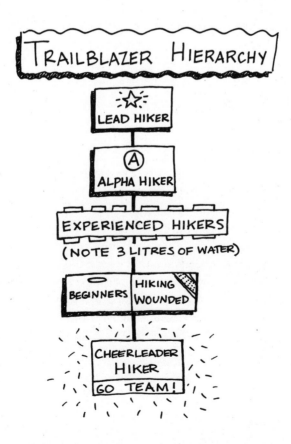

TRAILBLAZER HIERARCHY

LEAD HIKER

Ⓐ ALPHA HIKER

EXPERIENCED HIKERS
(NOTE 3 LITRES OF WATER)

BEGINNERS | HIKING WOUNDED

CHEERLEADER HIKER
GO TEAM!

We're so lucky to live 30 miles away from an International United Nations Biosphere Reserve, a place on par with the Everglades and the Galapagos Islands. It has 800-year-old trees, rare plants and animals, a complete unique ecology like no other on this planet.... Yes, the Niagara Escarpment.

The top is a windblown plateau, totally exposed to the vicissitudes of nature, wind, rain and snow from Lake Huron, where there's no soil and it's tough to grow anything except for a world-class hiking trail — the Bruce Trail.

There's a 350-foot limestone wall, 10,000-year-old moss and lichens in the nooks and crannies, 300-year-old pine trees white-knuckling on the ledges, and fallen rock, or tallis, at the bottom of the wall where the spring water bubbles up through the dense vegetation, cool and green.

And merrily meandering up and down the whole 400 miles from Niagara Falls to Tobermory is my old best pal, Bruce Trail. But how do I get there, Hiker Mike? How can I meet this Bruce fella for myself? Well, read on, gentle hiker.

WOLF COUNTRY

My friend Don Huff gave me a wonderful book called *Wolf Country*, about 11 years of tracking wolves in Algonquin Park. This amazing book is written by John and Mary Theberge, who spent more than 30 years doing field research on wolf-pack behaviour, especially in Algonquin Park. John's a professor of ecology at the University of Waterloo and one of the founders of the Kluane National Park in the Yukon. He and his wife go into the forest and make friends with a wolf pack, and through the use of radio collars they track the wolves and observe their behaviour over the years. *Wolf Country* is a fascinating read and is published by McClelland and Stewart.

Niagara Escarpment at the Rock Chapel Sanctuary

The best place to see the show is just north of Hamilton in the little town of Dundas at the Rock Chapel Sanctuary and Borer's Falls. Take the QEW to 403, north on Highway 6 to York Road West. Park in the North Shore Trails parking lot and you'll find the Bruce Trail markings just across the street. Borers Falls does just that, right over the Escarpment, and the Rock Chapel Sanctuary's got a maple-sugar shack. And you can hook up with the Armstrong Trail, but only in summer unless you're a courageous hiker, because it's too darn icy in winter. I love the Escarpment. The Rock Chapel Sanctuary and Borer's Falls are excellent holy places to worship at the altar of Mother Nature. Four stars. It was W. H. Auden who said, "Man needs escape as much as he needs food and deep sleep." So activate the escape hatch, hikers, and take a hike with Hiker Mike.

Glen Eden to Rattlesnake Point

Hikers, if you've ever driven west out the 401 towards Milton and Campbellville, and if you look to your left, you'll see the lakes and rivers, and downhill ski trails of Kelso and Glen Eden sitting astride the majestic Niagara Escarpment. A mecca for hikers, bikers, windsurfers, skiers and trout fishermen, with 15K of rugged Bruce Trail, well-marked and heading south to Rattlesnake Point, and some of the most inspiring vista and dangerous rock climbing in Ontario. Kelso, Glen Eden, Hilton Falls and Rattlesnake Point can all be easily reached by taking Highway 25 north from the 401. The way is so well marked, you can't get lost.

Inside Glen Eden, you'll pick up the white and blue blazes of the Bruce once you're through the railway tunnel in front of the ski chalet. Head up the mountain and into the bush, and ten breathless minutes later you're standing on top of the Escarpment next to the ski lift. This is a mountain biking centre, so keep an eye out and an ear open.

Just before you get to Rattlesnake you'll see the ground drop away dramatically into the Nasagawaya Canyon, but the Blue Bruce climbs the rockface straight up and continues along the high ledge. It's just you, bunky, and that 350-year-old cedar gazing fearfully over the precipice. The trail is rife with rocky outcroppings, so wear your sticky boots and please be careful. Danger stalks the cliffs at Rattlesnake. Climbers have perished on the rocks below, so stay well back while taking in the view.

Glen Eden to Rattlesnake Point is a four-hour, five-star Hiker Mike special. Best time to go is a weekday. You'll have it all to yourself — until ski season, of course. So put your boots to it, hikers. Hit the Kelso Comeback Trail and take a hike to Rattlesnake Point and back, for your health's sake.

HIKING PROTOCOL

Most hiking trails cross country roads, so if you keep an eagle eye open, you'll spot them heading off into the bush as you pass by in your car. And when you park at the trailhead, make sure you pull well off the road and try not to block the trail or infringe on private property. You don't want to anger landowners by being insensitive.

And speaking of hiker's protocol, here's a message from Linda Shephard about hiking manners on group hikes. "Last Sunday we joined the Oak Ridges Trail Club for an excellent hike. However, a small group hiked ahead of the leader, and in order that this group did not get too far ahead, the lead hiker had to increase his pace. From the very large gaps that developed, we concluded that the pace was too fast." Please, hikers, stay behind the hike leader. He knows the pace and distance and will make sure you enjoy the hike and arrive at trail's end in one piece.

Hilton Falls Secret Hike

Finally, hikers, I'm going to share with you my favourite secret Bruce Trail hike. You see, I used to live off Highway 25 out Milton way, north of the 401, high atop the Niagara Escarpment on a seldom-used section of the Bruce Trail just above Chudleigh's Apple Farm. But when CFRB called me back to Toronto and I had to leave my Hiker Hideout on the Bruce, my neighbours made me promise not to reveal the Hideout's where-abouts, for fear that hordes of Urban Sherpas would invade the peace and serenity that my neighbours have come to cherish. And Hiker Mike will not break his promise, but I'll tell you what I'm gonna do. I'm going to show you where the hike is, but we'll access it from a different entrance.

Follow the 401 west to Highway 25 north, and exactly 5 miles later you'll come to the 15 Sideroad. Turn left for a mile to the town line south. Turn left again and a half a mile later you'll come upon the Willowbrook Bed and Breakfast. Just across the street is the Bruce Trail and the 20K Hilton Falls loop, which will put you on the prettiest, roughest, rockiest and most challenging five-hour hike this side of Nepal's Annapurna Sanctuary. The trail is full of great rocky outcrops but is clearly marked with Bruce's blue blazes, and not only winds its way through Hilton Falls, home of a 10,000-year-old glacier lake, but takes you around one of the largest limestone quarries in Ontario by way of the rocky ridge, with views of Toronto 40 miles away. Wear really good hiking boots. Take a day to do this hike and bring a lot of food and water and, since this is my favourite secret hike, don't you dare breathe a word about it to anyone.

Legend and myth surround the old mill ruins at Hilton Falls. Gold has been found there in the deep limestone caverns. Stories have been passed down through the years that Hilton Falls was a stop on the Underground Railway, helping the American slaves to escape the United States in the 1850s. But hikers, beware of something very spooky. Sometimes you can find the falls and sometimes you can't. It's like Brigadoon. I've hiked through the

Hilton Falls wilderness a hundred times but I'll be double dog damned if I can find the Hilton Falls every time. Only the astute coureurs de bois will pick up the trail markings, and follow the path through the mist to where the Falls should be.

How to get there? Families can go directly to the Hilton Falls Park without taking the 20K hike. Drive 40 minutes west of Toronto on the 401 to Exit 312 on the Guelph Line and follow the signs to mysterious Hilton Falls.

30 Bruce Trail Bed and Breakfast

Y ou know when spring is here. You can feel it in the air and you can see it in the bush. The trails are still chock full of ice and snow and mud but it won't be long before it all dries up and we're doing the bushwhack dance again. And what better way to introduce you back to the Bruce Trail, close to town, than to hook you up with a hiker's bed and breakfast.

I always try to slip out of town midweek for a little boot, and this past Wednesday I headed west out the 401 to Milton and up Highway 25 onto the top of the Niagara Escarpment. I turned left — west — onto the 15 Sideroad and left again onto the Town Line south, to the Bruce Trail, and one of my favourite Bruce Trail hikes — the 20K Hilton Falls Side Trail.

Normally this is a five-hour hike at the best of times, but the trail was so bad, we only got a couple of hours under our belts before we gave up and headed back to the car on the Town Line. And there we happened by chance to bump into our old hiking pal, retired conservation teacher and bird guy Ron Hudson, who is now the proud owner of the beautiful Willowbrook Bed and Breakfast, right across the Town Line Road from the head of Bruce Trail. What a perfect place for a B&B, and it caters mainly to hikers.

Imagine returning to the Willowbrook after a five-hour hike and sliding your weary bones into the hot tub nestled in the cedars, then crawling between warm, clean sheets for a great night's sleep. Ron and Karen Hudson will pack a lunch for your hikes, show you the trails, and even come and pick you up from the trailhead when the hiking day is done. The en-suite double rooms with shower and television cost $65 a night with an extensive breakfast menu included. Sounds heavenly, eh, hikers? If this is your idea of civilized hiking, call Ron and Karen Hudson at Willowbrook Bed and Breakfast in Speyside at 905-876-1318.

31 Limehouse

Old pal Bruce Trail is such a gentleman. Anyone who hikes with Bruce will tell you that he takes excellent care of you. If the main trail is too rough and steep, and you and your dog can't climb the rockface, Bruce will take you around the difficulty on one of his blue-blazed side trails. Bruce will also make sure you get an eyeful of spectacular cliff-edge Escarpment vista, and deep and dark cedar river valleys. Bruce'll take you over turnstiles and farmer's fields, and detour you onto quiet country lanes. Bruce Trail is a most gracious and accommodating host. He's Hiker Mike's hero.

Take Limehouse, for instance, the little village that time forgot. Go up Trafalgar to Highway 7, west one concession to the Limehouse cutoff. Park in the centre of town beside the old stone Scout House and follow the white blazes south. And for a beautiful change of scene, take the blue-blazed Side Trail back to your car. Weekend campers set tents up on the ridge and down by the river. Hiking is heavenly. Thank you, Bruce.

Every time I hike the Bruce Trail, I feel grateful. It's only a half an hour from downtown Toronto; it's free; it's a well-marked, well-groomed, five-star, 420-mile trail running from Niagara Falls to Tobermory; and it's all ours, hikers. You don't have to be a member of the Bruce Trail Club to walk on the Bruce Trail but your annual $30 membership fee sure helps the different clubs with their trail building and maintenance. Members who maintain the trails are volunteers. They'll tell you which club is closest to you and they'll send you their quarterly magazine with great hiking articles and a list of upcoming events.

For an extra 30 bucks you can get the *Bruce Trail Reference Trail Guide and Map*, which is a plastic-covered ring-binder of some 50 or 60 maps, out of which you can take the appropriate map along on the hike with you. There's a little plastic wrapper that the map fits into, so as not to get it wet or full of dirt. It's well worth the $30 if you're going to do any serious hiking on the Bruce Trail. To join the Bruce Trail Association, call 1-800-665-HIKE and tell them Hiker Mike sent you.

If you like to hike the Bruce Trail on your own, do what I do. Head out the 401 to 25 north, towards Acton's Leathertown, and when you hit the 17 Sideroad at the top of the Escarpment, turn right and go to the end. That'll put you on the Speyside–Limehouse Bruce Trail tract. It's 5K to Limehouse and 5K back. Just look for the white blazes of the Bruce at road's end to lead your way.

The Great Esker Loop

This Sunday morning we are going to access the Great Esker Trail, just to the east of Trafalgar Road, off the 27 Sideroad, north of Georgetown. Most hikers start their trek from the Scottsdale Farm, where there's ample parking, but the Bruce Trail takes such a great loop around the property, it takes an hour and a half just to get to the Great Esker Loop. The same goes for trying to access the Esker from Limehouse to the south, so park your car on the 27 Sideroad and the 8th Line and there you'll find the Bruce Trail at Silver Creek.

Head south on the Bruce following the white blazes of the main trail and a short, ten-minute walk will take you to the blue blazes of the Great Esker Side Trail, high atop a section of the majestic Niagara Escarpment. Immediately you're surrounded by hundreds of large hummocks, mounds of high ground, covered with maple, oak and hickory hardwood, and by this time you may be asking, "What the hell is an esker, Hiker Mike?"

Esker is a Gaelic word. The Great Esker is a high, icy ridge of

10,000-year-old glacial deposit running like a great long dragon's tail, high above noisy and glistening Silver Creek. Gargantuan red pines, thick two-trunked 80-foot beasts some 12 feet in circumference, rule from on high. Then we topple down into the wide expanse of farmers' fields and newly planted white pines that couldn't be more than five or six years old.

The Great Esker is a well-travelled path that leads you onto a mountain crest looking to the south and east, all the way down to Lake Ontario; it's an amazing panorama that must be seen. The Great Esker will spill you onto the steep and deserted 8th Line, which is closed for the winter — a toboggan run that goes straight up into the sky leading you back to the 27 Sideroad and your car in less than two hours time. It's an arduous climb, hikers, and next time, goll-darnit, I'm bringing a toboggan. On which my big lard-ass will sit. And I'll go for the ride of a lifetime!

WHAT'S IN MY BACKPACK?

1. Folded-up rubberized poncho, foul-weather gear on the bottom. Good to wear in the rain and sleet, or build a shelter if you're lost in the forest.

2. Bungee cord ties the poncho down and doubles as a leash for Rupert in those environmentally sensitive areas.

3. Litre of water and Leatherman All-Purpose Tool.

4. Extra socks for when you get a soaker.

5. Couple of chocolate bars and an orange.

6. Big plastic bag to keep your backpack dry in case of rain or to pick up Rupert's poop.

7. And don't forget your hat and gloves.

8. But most important, pack your cell phone just in case you get lost, hikers, or break your leg.

9. If you've got room, Coke, Mars Bar and rolling papers for the halfway Coke-and-a-smoke break.

Wanna lose some holiday weight? Put a brick in your backpack and take it for a hike too. Makes a great workout.

Scottsdale Farm

G ot a good, rugged up-and-down, four-season hike for all you coureurs de bois out there. This trek will renew your joy of hiking. Jump right in your car, and drive the 401 west to Trafalgar Road north past Highway 7, to Scottsdale Farm — 1,300 hectares of fields and river valleys on the Niagara Escarpment, donated to the Ontario Heritage Foundation back in 1982 by Stewart and Violet Bennett. The Scottsdale has been a working farm for over 200 years, so keep Bowser on a leash and stay away from the domestic animals, okay? The Bruce Trail winds through the property along with the Bennett Heritage Trail. They're both well marked and groomed.

A walk around the property will take you two hours. Add on the 4K Great Esker Loop at the bottom of the Bennett, and the whole kit 'n' kaboodle will take you four hours. You're going to see something pretty special on the Bennett Trail. On the south-facing slopes of the river valleys, you'll see Carolinian vegetation — trees and shrubs that normally grow a lot further south, say Carolina — lots of oak, pine and blueberry, walnut and sugar maple. This hike is great for kids and parents.

We've been hiking regularly with my old buddy, Bruce Trail. Once a month on a Sunday morning, we do a segment of the Bruce with two cars, one of which we place at the end of the hike — about 12 to 15 miles away. That way we don't have to double back to our starting point. These hikes take us about four hours all in, snack break included!

Alton Main Street Hike

W e set out last Sunday morning to hike the Forks of the Credit from the Devil's Pulpit in Belfountain, down into the Forks of the Credit River Valley, and up the Cataract Bruce Trail north to

Alton, and lunch at the Millcroft Inn. Well, we started out okay...

We left Hiker Hideout at 6:30 am to the sounds of Donabie on CFRB, and arrived in Alton to leave the first car. It was supposed to be a two-car hike, but it took us another hour to find the darned Bruce Trail, which ran down the main street of Alton, blue blazes on the telephone posts and on the side wall of the General Store. You see, we didn't do our map work ahead of time, so we were ill-prepared in making a start, and as a result didn't have enough time to take the other car back to the Devil's Pulpit. So we just walked the Alton Bruce Trail section south to Highway 24 and that was cool. Took us about 1½ hours through meadow and field, maple ridge and riverside down through the cedar valley. A-1. Silk purse out of a pig's butt. We were lucky after all.

With the Bruce Trail running down the Main Street of Alton, hikers, it doesn't matter which direction you choose to get out of town. Either way heads into the bush. As Yogi Berra used to say, "When you come to the fork in the road, take it!" My choice? Head north and west to Big Hill — a good climb in any hiker's book: a kind of table mountain overlooking the town. Directions to Alton: up Highway 10 north to Caledon, then left (west) on 24 to Coulterville and left on 136 north to Alton's main crossroads. Go to the Caledon Inn for lunch but take a bag of money with you. Great wine cellar. Hike on!

35 Glen Haffy Autumn Hike

There is a very special place not far from Toronto where two giant landmasses come together and you can hike the Dingle right down the middle. The Dingle is a small, narrow, wooded valley with the mammoth gravel humps and bumps of the Oak Ridges Moraine on the one side of you and the Great Northeast Deciduous Forest of the Niagara Escarpment looming ever larger on the other. And I'm walking the Glen Haffy tightrope right down the middle!

Glen Haffy is the picture-perfect postcard called Christmas!

Snow falling on cedars in the mountains. Follow the blue blazes of the Bruce Trail past a little old schoolhouse built in 1872 and on into Glen Haffy Park, but beware the dark pine forest. The paths wind through with no rhyme or reason and it's too cloudy to see the sun or the blue blazes of the Bruce, and you'll soon be hollerin' "Where in the blue blazes are we?"

The easy way to get to Glen Haffy would be to go up the Airport Road and 45 minutes later you drive in the front gates just south of Highway 9; and I recommend just that for families and seniors. But for you coureurs de bois — you know who you are — head up Highway 50 to Highway 9, turn left, then west to Glen Haffy Road south. Park your car when the snow stops you — Glen Haffy Road turns into the blue blazes of the Bruce Trail. You're not going to get a better four-seasons hike than Glen Haffy, and where else can you sing and dance "Down in the Dingle"?

Caledon and Credit River Hikes

HIKER + MIKE'S
SURVIVAL KIT:

◦ 3 litres of water
* Snowshoes
◦ Sturdy Shoes
(with cushy insides)
\$ Enough \$ for
a modest lunch
(pickled egg and can
of coke – minimum)
↓↓essential↓↓↙
◦ Charged up cell phone

36 The Devil's Pulpit

The Fountain of Youth lives on in the old village of Belfountain, tucked away in a tiny little park under the Devil's Pulpit sitting high atop Caledon Mountain, and legend has it that the hiker who walks down into Belfountain for lunch every day then back up the mountain to sleep every night shall have a long and happy life. The Bruce Trail pathway leaps over the Devil's Pulpit at the top of the mountain, and then catapults hundreds and hundreds of feet into the Forks of the Credit Valley below. A rocky limestone staircase descends into a suicide series of ropes and handrails anchored to giant pines and cedar. Just below the railway tracks you'll come upon a mossy grotto full of fairy greenery amid a jumble of giant boulders, out of which blows a blast of Mother Nature's air-conditioning. You see, hikers, deep down under the Escarpment runs the Credit River, and the energy created by the rushing river sends a water-cooled wind upward through the rocks, so you can sit and cool down from your uphill Bruce Trail hike on your journey back to the top of the Pulpit.

It's ironic that there's no more beautiful section of the Bruce Trail than Belfountain but it's almost impossible to find the trail, it's so hidden away. It's not easy to spot from the Forks of the

"The Devil's Pulpit made me do it."
—HIKER MIKE—
(with apologies to Flip Wilson.)

Credit Road, unless you stop at the Forks Bridge and search for the white blazes, so the best place to pick up the Bruce is at the top of the Grange Sideroad above Belfountain, one concession east of Mississauga Road. Leave your car there, hike north to the Pulpit, down into the Forks through the little 1800s village of Brimstone, and on up into the Forks of the Credit Provincial Park and those world-famous waterfalls where the Silurian and the Ordovician Land Masses collided 400 million years ago. Remember? That's our halfway spot for the hike. Let's say three hours roundtrip, hikers, and you'll never want to leave. The Credit Valley will steal your heart away. The Ojibwa believed that the Forks was the home of their god, Manitou. Best time for a Belfountain hike is midweek. Never go in autumn, because the antique shoppers and leaf gawkers jam up the roads in the village and the paths in the forest.

37 Belfountain: Trimble Trail

For those of you who do not wish to jump over the Pulpit, a safer place to access the Bruce is on the Forks of the Credit Road where the old cement bridge crosses the river and heads north into Brimstone and the provincial park beyond. But the real Fountain of Youth actually exists, folks, in the little Belfountain Conservation Park, tucked under Main Street across from the Belfountain Inn. You'll see the gates right beside the river. Park your car and discover a hundred-year-old estate, complete with manicured grounds, stone canals, cannons, caves, grottoes and waterfalls, and the Fountain of Youth itself. And right behind it is the beginning of the Trimble Trail, a gentle and well-groomed pathway leading down to the Forks, passing under the Giant Pulpit of the Devil looming ominously overhead.

One way to the Forks — half an hour, tops. A magical and manageable dance through the forest for kids and grandmas. Belfountain is as close as Southern Ontario comes to Canmore in

Alberta's Kananaskis Country — the perfect Rocky Mountain River Valley right here, an hour north of Toronto. Take the 401 to Mississauga Road north to "La Belle Fontaine de la Jeunesse."

38 Belfountain: Forks of the Credit

When the leaves are starting to change in the Great Northeastern Deciduous Forest, that means it's time to leave the old ecological niche and dance into the woods to celebrate the changing of the colour guard. And there is no better place to go for this than where the Niagara Escarpment meets Belfountain and the Forks of the Credit River. This magical little valley tucked under its own mountain is so beautiful that we've got two hikes for you.

For those of you with families and pets who want a little more control and regularity on your hikes, head on up Highway 10 to Highway 24 and the Forks of the Credit Provincial Park. Highways 10 and 24. The Meadow Hike past the Glacier Lake to the ancient falls (163 stair steps down) and back to the parking lot takes about an hour, and the waterfall is fantastic. The meeting of the limestone of the Silurian and the red clay strata of the Ordovician is very much in evidence at the Falls. Highway 10 and turn left on 24 and you're there.

For you coureurs de bois who prefer the road less travelled: Just as you're coming into Belfountain on Mississauga Road, you'll see the big blue Belfountain sign on the right. Turn left immediately into an old deserted farm, complete with barn foundation and silo. Park in the barnyard and follow the tractor trail south for miles and miles into the maples, oaks and pine forests. Walk out for an hour or so, have a picnic, and hike on back to the car. Cold drinks and coffee in Belfountain at the Village Store when the long trek is over.

Both hikes are 45 minutes from downtown T.O., so hike in the morning and pick up some apples in the afternoon at the Apple Factory on Mississauga Road just to the south at Highway 7.

39 Terra Cotta

The ancient city of Katmandu, Nepal, sits at the crossroads of two of the oldest caravan trails in the world. The north-south trail from Tibet to India bisects the east-west silk route from China to Venice. And right here in Southern Ontario, we have Terra Cotta, the land of red earth. And hiking in the Credit River Valley at Terra Cotta reminds me of hiking in the Himalayan foothills: all pines and rhododendrons. The mountains aren't as big, but the trails that cross each other are better maintained and boy, oh boy, do we have a choice of hikes — the Credit Valley Footpath, the Bruce Trail, the Caledon Trailway, the Belfountain and the Terra Cotta Conservation Areas.

The ultimate four-season hike lies only 40 minutes west of Toronto on the 401 at the top of Winston Churchill Boulevard. You can park at the Terra Cotta Inn and hike the Credit Valley Footpath right beside the river; or you can hike to the Conservation Area and pick up the Bruce Trail for a two-hour walk in the park, more suitable for families and beginner hikers who need a little more definition to their forest forays.

Because towns like Katmandu and Terra Cotta lie at the crossroads, they normally have restaurants from every country in the world, but this is where my whimsical comparison blows up in my face. The Terra Cotta Inn is the only restaurant, but it works just fine if you're hungry. Just take some dough, hikers, cause it ain't cheap. Hikers Dave and Mike had only enough money for a Coke and a pickled egg, but that's a good lunch for a coupla guys from the Golden Horseshoe! You'll not find a more beautiful river valley than the Credit at Terra Cotta. The perfect hike? I'm thinking so.

40 Credit Valley Conservation Area

Winter hiking in Orangeville and Terra Cotta. We've been waiting for it, hikers, and now we've got it. In spades. Snow. We can slap the snowshoes onto our hiking boots, or get out the cross-country skis and toboggans and the whole fam damily can head for the hills — the Albions, the Caledons, and the Oak Ridges — for whole weekends of fun. And here are a few suggestions for you outdoor people in the Greater Toronto area.

My friend Karen just called to let everyone know that the Credit Valley Conservation Area in Orangeville is open for business, along with the Terra Cotta Conservation Area, up at the top of Winston Churchill Boulevard, just north of Highway 7. Karen gave me a partial list of activities they've been enjoying up in the snowy Caledon Hills. Hiking, snowshoeing trails are open, along with tobogganing and cross-country skiing, ice fishing, birdwatching, and for you hardy souls — winter camping. *Brrrrr!*

And all you do to get the winter festivities started is give Karen a phone call at Island Lake in Orangeville at 519-941-6329, and Marébeth Switzer at the Terra Cotta Credit Valley main number, 905-670-1615, extension 240. They're both really nice and very helpful. I've always said, "Dance with Mother Nature and she'll clasp you to her bosoms," but with some of the snowfalls we've been given lately, it seems like less of a clasping and more like a good spanking.

41 Credit Valley Footpath

For you coureurs de bois out there who are in great shape, try the Credit Valley Footpath from Terra Cotta to Norval and back — well, almost. It's three hours of the most rigorous ups and downs along the valley walls — not along the Credit River — oh, no. That would be too easy. The Credit Valley Footpath is a thousand-year-old Ojibwa trail. The ups and downs are relentless but the terrain is so biodiversified, you keep passing through different ecosystems — everything from lowland jungle full of fern and wildflower to Carolinian forest sun-pockets to high pasture meadow. It'll blow your mind and your lungs. Your legs'll scream for mercy.

After about an hours' hiking south on the Credit, you'll come to the old Stone Mill Ruins — a great turn-around picnic spot. Now, just past the ruins is what I call a mugwump. You run down a steep, short hill really fast and then up the other side without stopping. The path is muddy and covered with leaves and ice — sorta slippery! It's a "trust yourself" kinda thang, like tight-roping on a log over a raging river.

Only one problem, hikers. You've got to turn around at the Old Mill ruins just north of UCC Norval Campus and head back, because UCC has closed its property to hikers and you can't pass through any more. I guess renegade bikers and ATV and four-wheel-drive guys messed it up for us. So park your car at the southwest corner of the 10th Line and Halton Hills 22nd Sideroad just west of Terra Cotta, and test your hiking mettle. Jump the turnstile and head southeast along the Bruce Trail blue section down to the ruins and back — three hours of rough and tough. The Credit Valley Footpath rocks. Hike on!

COLD COMFORT

From my old pal Don Gautier, who just happens to be an honorary Algonquin chief, and all-round bull-shooter. Chief Don offers this advice to hikers who find themselves trapped in deep snow: Lie down flat on your stomach and roll over and over back toward where you came from. The same works for deep slush on a not-so-frozen lake. I wish I knew this remedy last year up on Lake Temagami when I started to sink up to my thighs into the slush that once was ice. I was so scared that I just up and walked on water back to shore. Another good tip for hikers whose hands get cold. Take off your gloves and shove your hands down the front of your pants next to your skin. Works for guys and gals, and makes you feel good all over, besides.

Caledon Trailway
Palgrave to Terra Cotta

The weather has been changing from cold and ice to warm and wet so much lately, I wasn't sure which hike to do last Sunday morning. Credit River Valley was out of the question — too spongy and very under water — but we still wanted to do the Caledons, so I phoned Julie at Canoe Country and Bruce Trail Guides in Norval (905-846-5000), because she knows the trails better than Hiker Mike, and I asked her. So she says, "How'd ya like a hike through the Caledon Hills without going up and down the hills yourself? Yes? Then the Caledon Trailway is the hike for you." The Trailway is an old railway line that runs for 22 miles between Palgrave on Highway 50 way over to Terra Cotta at the top of Winston Churchill Road — don't worry about trains coming — the rail tracks have been removed! The Niagara Escarpment, the Credit and the Humber River Valleys, the Caledons and Albion Hills are all the bailiwick of the Caledon Trailway, soon to be part of the Trans Canada Trail.

So flat, smooth and beautiful, the Trailway's good for seniors, families and even wheelchair hikers, but you coureurs de bois can test your cardiovasculars by seeing how fast you can go over a given distance. You see, hikers, with every concession road you cross, the Caledon Trailway gives you the exact distance, so you can time yourself on the way out and compare it with your time on the way back. So hit the Comeback Trail to fitness. It won't be long before the old bathing suit comes out of the drawer. Remember what you tried to stuff into it last year? Don't let that happen again! Not a pretty sight. Take a Trailway hike and watch the fat melt off of your you-know-what.

Caledon Trailway Hike #1: I walked from Old Church Road off Highway 50 to the Patterson Sideroad in 50 minutes, including stop time to write my comments as I went, but full out, it only took me 40 minutes to get back to the car.

Caledon Trailway Hike #2: We left one car at the Terra Cotta Inn and the other at the Inglewood Fire Station, some 6 or 7 miles away, and off we went. A good straight walk through the Caledon Hills, surrounded on all sides by the farms and chalets of the swanky Caledon set. Get your maps out and find Terra Cotta north of Highway 7 at the top of Winston Churchill. It's a four-hour call, so take a Saturday or Sunday morning and lunch at the Terra Cotta Inn.

Caledon Trailway Hike #3: Up Highway 50 past Bolton, past the Albion Hills entrance, turn left on Patterson Sideroad and shazaam, the Caledon Trailway crosses the road. What a beautiful old railway it must have been. The trail of cinder stretches out endlessly, covered in a carpet of yellow and red wildflowers and purple heather, through forest and farm into the mystic. And take your radio with you, tune it to CFRB, and you'll be amazed how quickly the time goes while hiking and listening.

You don't have to be a hiker to do the Caledon Trailway. Just put on a pair of sturdy shoes, cushy on the inside, of course, and walk your way to fitness. We're all going to live a lot longer than we expect, hikers, so let's be in reasonable shape to enjoy it.

43 Albion Hills

Albion Hills is the first conservation area in Ontario, hikers. It sits high atop the Oak Ridges Moraine, a two-million-year-old glacial watershed that brings Toronto its drinking water by way of the Humber, the Rouge, the Don River and Highland Creek. The Oak Ridges Moraine is a long ribbon of sand and gravel stretching east to Peterborough and west to the Niagara Escarpment.

The Albions and the Caledons were reforested in the 1940s with a million pine trees. Albion Hills is a great three-hour hike on the Red Trail in the late fall, with dazzling overviews of the Caledons, and mushy, wet cedar river valleys, all the while hiking on groomed and grassy pathways 10 feet wide. Hiker Heaven, Batman. Now, something wacky and wonderful happened on our hike last Sunday. After some pretty rigorous going on the Red

Trail, we got back to the car to find that we'd been locked in — big iron gate blocking our exit. So we hiked down to the main gate. Nobody home. Uh-oh. I got out my cell phone and called Metro Conservation Authority at 416-661-6600, and a nice lady named Gail told us to go back to our car. Larry, the Parks guy, was on his way to let us out.

And so, a great big tip of the hiker hat to the folks at the Metro Conservation Authority and also to Bell Mobility for the use of the cell phone. 'Cuz in this instance, help was only a phone call away.

Albion Hills: 401 west — 427 north — 50 north, past Bolton on the left side of Highway 50. Everybody welcome — kids and grandmas, coureurs de bois, and guerrillas — to 26K of trails for hiking and cross-country skiing. This is a four-hour call. Stop in at Tim Hortons on 50 south of Bolton on your way home for a large regu and a bagel à la cinnamon raisin.

Oak Ridges Hikes

Running across the top of our Megacity from the Caledons in the west, to Glen Major north of Pickering in the east, is the mighty Oak Ridges Moraine, those great huge humps and bumps of sand and gravel under which percolate the headwaters of the Toronto Basin, the Credit, the Humber, the Don, the Rouge and the Duffins. And dancing through the forest on top of the whole she-bang is the Oak Ridges Trail. And she's a beauty, hikers. And here are a few rules the Trail Association asks us to follow while hiking:

1. Stay on the trail.
2. Keep dogs on a leash.
3. Protect trees and crops and wildlife.
4. Use stiles to cross the fences.
5. Carry all litter out. Remember, hikers, if you pack it in, you must pack it out. (All except for you-know-what, and there I draw the line!)
6. Take nothing but photographs and leave nothing but your footprints.

The trail-user's guide is kind of a metaphor for life, don't you think, hikers? Happy Harold Sellers, Oak Ridges trailblazer, just sent me the new "Oak Ridges Trail Guide," full of detachable maps for routes from Caledon to Clarington, a cultural history of the trail, and first-aid tips for hikers. Call 1-877-319-0284 for your copy.

WINTER ROAD HIKES

Let's talk about backcountry winter road hikes in which you hike around the big square of a country concession. It's best to stay out of the bush this time of the year. Too treacherous and icy. So, just because the sun's out and the weather is starting to get a little warmer, don't be fooled into thinking you can wear your sneakers on country-road walks. These roads are very muddy, so keep to your extreme winter hiking boots.

44 Oak Ridges Trail, Aurora

Head on up Bathurst Street, north of Aurora's Bloomington Sideroad, and turn west along the 16th Concession, and there you'll find the Oak Ridges Trailhead, wonderfully busy this time of year (we counted 16 cars in the hikers' parking lot). The trail runs west through some of the most magnificent estates in the Toronto area, starting just across Dufferin with Eaton Hall, a French stone chateau with sculptured grounds and a lake filled with a million ducks and geese who can't decide whether to fly south this year or not. Then, across Keele, we happen upon the Mary Lake Estate of the Augustinian Fathers, complete with marshes, church, retreat house and shrine all the way over to Highway 400, where we took a lunch break before heading back. There are only a couple of steep hills, and the path is flat and soft and wide, so the whole hike will take you four hours back to your car.

Thank you, landowners, for letting the Oak Ridges Trail cross your land. We hikers will never let you down. Hikers are poets, not vandals. Thanks to Bill Roberts, Peter Attfield, Fiona Cowles, Bob Ellison and the gang on the Oak Ridges Trail for a great hiking experience. And if you live up that way, hikers, why not join the trail club? Write to ORTA, Box 28544, Aurora, Ontario, L46 6S6, or phone 416-410-2601 for membership.

45 Oak Ridges Trail West

Ou sont les neiges d'antan? the French poet François Villon once asked. Where are the snows of yesteryear, hikers? Well, they put in an appearance north of Highway 7 last weekend, and though the snows didn't stay for long, they reminded me that the snows of tomorrow will soon be here for another long Canadian winter. The trails we have come to rely upon for our hiking will

soon be inundated with the white stuff and impassable without snowshoes. And speaking of snowshoes, I just bought a pair of Fat Louies, made in Village Huron, Quebec. They're like giant French tennis rackets strung with catgut, with little leather straps to go around my hiking boots. Got 'em on now. I practise around the house when Mrs. Mike goes shopping, but I stay mostly on the rugs. The Fat Louies scratch the hardwood floors.

Hiker Mike's winter hike of choice begins on the Caledon King Town Line and the 19 Sideroad, the west extension of the Oak Ridges Trail — 32K of Oak Ridges Trail in King Township alone. Thirty-two! Now the beauty of this country road hike is, the rich people live up this section of the Caledons, so no matter how hard it snows and blows, you know the roads will be plowed *tout de suite* — that's French for quick as a New York minute — so you can hike with impunity when the bush is full of snow.

Directions to Oak Ridges Trail West: Park one car at the 8th Concession north of 17 Sideroad, and the other at Caledon King Town Line and 19 Sideroad. Hike for 9 miles of Caledon roads in between. Lots of ups and downs. Your heart will thank you about 180 times per minute. It's a good idea to keep this roadside winter boot in your back pocket. Pull it out when your pants get too tight because of that ever-expanding holiday backside.

46 Bruce's Mill, Stouffville

Hikers, if you're looking for a great hike and you don't mind a little car noise, then head on up the 404, which is the Don Valley Parkway extension north, to the Stouffville Road, and just east of Warden is Bruce's Mill.

Right inside the gates you'll find the orange, red and yellow trails, which will take you into the big maple forest. Go hungry, hikers, because there's a pancake house and sugar shack right on the trail. Smack dab in the middle of Bruce's Mill are two streams, a beautiful lake with a sandy beach, and waterfall for swimming. Heaven on toast. Trail-wise, you've got to use your head and trust your sense of direction, because it gets a little confusing. Farmer's fields break up the path. But use the sun as your guide, and when in doubt, keep to the outside fence.

And just when you think you're hopelessly lost, you come out of the plowed furrows and into a massive and mowed grassy park a hundred acres in size, full of picnic tables and dandelions. You could make a day of it if you include some fishing, swimming,

BE PREPARED TO STRIP & STASH

Hikers, every autumn we move into the cold and wet part of the year, so let's talk about hiking attire. The secret to comfortable hiking is layering your clothing. Next to the skin is a cotton long-sleeved turtleneck, covered by a synthetic fleece or wool sweater. Then a Gore-Tex shell with a hood for wind and rain and finally, for the below-zero days, add a light down parka. Cotton, fleece, Gore-Tex and down. You see, hikers, as you heat up on the hike, strip off a layer and stash it in your backpack. Even your down coat will squinch up into a little ball in the bottom. Another helpful hint from your Urban Sherpa. Check out www.hikermike.com for more information about hiking gear in the Tried-and-True Hall of Fame page on the Hiker Mike website.

pancakes and maple syrup along with your hiking. If you need a great spot for a family picnic or reunion, this is it. Call Gail at Metro Conservation at 416-661-6600 for reservations. Great hike for seniors and families. Costs $4 for adults, $3 for seniors, $2 for kids. Bruce's Mill is light and airy, nothing scary. Your grandma will love it. Just don't forget to take her home with you when you leave. *Carpe diem,* hikers. Seize the day.

47 Whitchurch Conservation Area

I was rooting around the Oak Ridges Moraine, up on the Aurora Sideroad east of Woodbine and Warden last fall, when I happened upon the Whitchurch Conservation Area — and something wonderful happened. While I was hiking, the magical autumn wind came up out of the northwest and blew all the leaves off the trees and invited the sky into the bush for the winter once again. And I watched it happen, while hiking in Whitchurch. Nice little parking lot off Aurora Road with a sign full of rules, the best being "Take nothing with you and leave only your footprints," and before I was through I left two hours' worth.

Once inside the gate, stay to the left along the fence and you'll come upon a beautiful horse farm filled with Thoroughbred and quarter horses, elegant chateau backyards, and a series of deer pens that'll send your dog into a tizzy. This wide and gentle path will carry you into the York Regional Forest, Robinson Tract, and just before you complete the big circle you'll come upon a lake and grassy bank with a rain shelter and outhouse — perfect for a picnic.

Whitchurch hiking area is sweet and rustic, full of oak and pine, maple and cedar, and I'll long remember being at Whitchurch that magical day when the wind came up and blew all the leaves off the trees. Take 404 to Aurora Road East, past Warden to Whitchurch. So, moms, dads, kids and grandpas, take your pleasure, but leave only your footprints.

48 Jefferson Forest

My pal Paul from CFRB sales came up to me in the hallowed halls not long ago and told me about a hiking spot up the 404 Don Valley Parkway and west on Stouffville Road, almost to Bayview. And so with the afternoon free, I jump in the car and up into the Oak Ridges Moraine I go.

Well, good old Paul was right again as usual. Across the Stouffville Road from Trailwood Crescent, just east of Bayview, there is a parking lot and a gate, and heading down into the maple bush is every hiker's dream — a deep and wide and well-used trail disappearing into the mystic forest, heading north with adventure at every turn. No sooner was I on the journey when I bumped into a couple of local guys drinking coffee and walking their dogs. They grew up hiking these Gormley Stouffville trails and they were sad to tell me that the Powers That Be have seen fit to join up the dots and run the last unfinished section of Bayview Avenue right through the middle of the forest.

There you go, hikers — Great Cosmic Message — get up there and hike the Jefferson Forest tract without delay. Up on the top of the forest there are many private properties and signs along the east-west fencing that dead-ends the northbound trail. Don't even think of trespassing, hikers. Looks as if the landowner had some problems with vandals, so let's respect the signs and maybe he'll open up the trail again one day.

You'll soon come into the Jefferson Forest section on the northeast quarter of the landmass. Steep slopes, erodable soil, sensitive plants and animals, so no bikes, no horses, no motorized vehicles (which I think may have been that landowner's problem, what with dirt bikes and four-wheel drives), only hikers allowed. This Jefferson Forest Tract is a great little find. Stouffville Road just east of Bayview, hikers. Hit the Comeback Trail to Fitness, but hurry!

49 Greenwood: A Great Doggy Hike

Greenwood Conservation Area north of Ajax is doggy heaven, hikers. Millions of canines running free. Pile Bowser in the back of your car and head out the 401 East to Westney Road north of Ajax, to Greenwood Road West, and park by the gatehouse. Once inside, follow the park drive to the Duffins Trail sign — the beginning of a 4K loop that takes you riverside north high up into the hills. The trail is exceedingly well marked with black arrows burnt into bright red posts. The ups and downs are gentle enough for families and seniors with some experience, and along the top of the trail there are rustic tree-hewn benches upon which to sit and rest and contemplate the vista that Mother Nature has so generously given us.

The trail loops back through the woods, but coureurs de bois can keep to the river and hike further north through the gravel pit, where you'll find a bridge and abutment leading down to the river. Because of serious erosion, you'll find the rest of the bridge in a heap on the bottom of the river. This is a great spot for

fishing, swimming and camping. It's also a good lunch stop before heading back home, but when the riverside path disappears into the muck, time to take off your boots and socks, hike up your pants and cross the shallows, or find a log to tightrope your way to the east side because that's where the path continues. Even if you fall in, the water's only a foot deep. So take a chance, hikers, and have some fun. Heaven for hikers and doggies alike.

50 Goodwood: Oak Ridges Moraine

The Goodwood Conservation area is just to the north and east of Stouffville. The best way to get to it from downtown Toronto is to go straight up the 404 and across the Bloomington Sideroad east to Highway 47 to the little village of Goodwood. Turn right, head south on the 3rd Concession exactly 2 miles. The gate is on the right. If you see the Hyla Farm on the left you've gone too far. Go back immediately or you'll turn into a frog. The trail leading west into Goodwood is a well-marked section of the Oak Ridges Trail. Five minutes into the adventure we come down into a valley and the cedar-lined Duffins Creek complete with storybook bridge donated by Shell Canada's Environmental Fund. Good on you, Shell.

Once across the bridge you'll climb high up into a cedar bush filled with white and red pine. That spills you out into a high plain with an open field, and in the middle of that wide expanse sits a solitary iron water-pump marking the site of an ancient homestead. And as far as the eye can see, ringing this massive playing field of the gods, is the inexorable "march of the hundred thousand pines" south to the valley below. Goodwood has plentiful wildlife, including a large herd of deer. I've seen numerous animal paths crossing the Oak Ridges Trail, and when I reach the top, I notice there is a lot of deer poop on the southeastern slope of the hills — this is because the sun has burnt off the snow, revealing the tender grass for the deer to munch for their midwinter salad.

Just before coming to the 2nd Concession, there is an Oak Ridges sign asking us please to stay on the trail and keep our dogs leashed as we are about to re-enter civilization. Everything about the Oak Ridges Trail is gracious. The volunteers run their scenic and very challenging trails through a variety of ecosystems. Goodwood is a stunningly beautiful golden walk with loads of high ups and downs, through great pine forests and cedar swamps, rivers and floodplain. Five-star. The 2000 Golden Boot Award for the Best Damn Hike. Now, it's a fairly arduous hike but a great way to get rid of that large caboose sticking out behind you, so take a Goodwood hike for your fanny's sake.

51 Heberdown

Right behind Weall and Cullen Gardens on Country Lane just north of Whitby is Mark Cullen's secret hiking grounds, called Heberdown. It's like taking a hike in the Black Forest in Germany — deep, dark woods and high, wide sandy roads with great sweeping views of the Oak Ridges. If you follow the well-marked yellow signs to the Iroquois Shores Lookout, you'll have to go into the Devil's Den, way down into a valley filled with an island lake surrounded by thick woods and river bridges.

Back in the 1860s, horse thieves would camp in the valley overnight to water their horses, and the noise and racket the bandits made scared the locals so badly, they believed it was the devil himself. The Red Trail — Devil's Den Nature Trail — is a good family hike. The Orange Trail is a good boot through the woods for the coureurs de bois. And the 10K Yellow Trail takes you once more around the park, hikers. Three hours. Make your own path. Not for the faint of heart.

Heberdown can be reached by taking the 401 east to Highway 12 north, west on Taunton Road past Weall and Cullen, and north on Country Lane. Drop in and say hi to Gardener Mark. Tell him Hiker Mike sent you.

Humber River Hikes

About 12,000 years ago, indigenous peoples lived, hunted, travelled and traded their wares along the Humber River from Lake Ontario north to the Holland River and Georgian Bay, stalking the migrating herds for food, trading copper from Lake Superior for tools, shells from the Gulf of Mexico, and slate from the Maritimes. Some 300 villages and campsites have been discovered along the shores of the Humber. But the popularity of the Humber Trail was guaranteed when Etienne Brûlé and his hardy and courageous coureurs de bois discovered the Humber as a canoe portage for the burgeoning fur trade. Their boundless spirit helped our country grow. No one has time these days to hike the entire Humber River, but what weekend hikers can do is chop it up into hikeable sections and enjoy the great Carrying Place Trail at our leisure.

HIKING GEAR

When I talk about hiking gear, I mean a good sturdy pair of hiking boots, not ordinary sneakers. I wear Salomon Extreme hikers and Merrell Steel Blades. Both of these boot brands need little or no break-in time. Strap 'em on and hit the trail. Also, get yourself a lightweight waterproof LoweAlpine Triple Point Ceramic jacket for wind and rain, and in cool weather, a nice warm fleece to go under the jacket. Best to layer your clothes and adjust to the weather as it happens. Bring a water bottle and a snack if you're going to be away longer than a few hours. I like to take along a change of SmartWool socks to refresh my feet halfway though the hike. Or in case I get a soaker!

52 Eglinton to Lake Ontario

The first good Humber River Hike runs from Scarlet Flats on Eglinton Avenue east of Jane Street on down past the Old Mill at Bloor to Lake Ontario. It's 10K in 2½ hours. Hikers with kids and dogs take the bicycle path down the west bank. Coureurs de bois follow the river path down the east bank.

First you'll come to the Scarlet Woods Golf Club. Stay the heck off the greens and watch out for the goose poop. Fight to stay on the river path. It's worth it. No need to trespass the golf course, though. Cross the river to the west-side path; then the golfers won't shoot their balls at you. You'll discover the magic forest of gigantic gnarly willows, right out of the Wizard of Oz. Only once do you have to leave the Humber River. The west path forces you out onto Stephen Drive and the Stonegate Mall where you gotta stop into the Polish Donut Shop for a ponchkey, the most delicious Ukrainian donut you ever tasted. Before you know it, you're standing on the Humber River Bridge, looking out over Lake Ontario.

You can also access Etienne Brûlé Park and the Carrying Place Portage by jumping off the Bloor Subway at the Old Mill Station. Ask TTC Joan, the token taker, for directions. She works weekends.

53 Black Creek Pioneer Village

I'm back at Hiker Haven, my friends, sitting with my feet up in front of a roaring fire, recovering from yesterday's hike. The weather was so beautiful, I started a hike at 9 am and didn't get home until dinnertime, and I'm still numb from the waist down. But what a hike! Where was I? I'm gonna make you guess, Backpack Trivia style. Ready?

Return with us now to yesteryear when life moved at a different pace. Listen to the hollow clip-clop clopping of horses' hooves over the Old Mill Bridge. Smell the fresh-baked bread, stroll the wooden sidewalks, and experience life as it was 200 years ago. Where was I?

Black Creek Pioneer Village is on Steeles Avenue just east of Jane, south of Murray Ross Parkway. Entrance is on the west side and there's plenty of parking. South of the village you pick up the path along the Black Creek as it meanders through the Jane-Finch Corridor to Derrydowns Park and Northwood Park just north of Sheppard, and back to the Village. You can make it a two-hour walk, but I don't recommend it in winter. My hiking buddy Gary Beechey, the official photographer of CFRB, says, "This is a great place to hike in summer but you'll break your neck this time of year." The trail is pure ice, so come back and try it in the spring.

The Black Creek Valley is private and pretty but it is also the backyard to hundreds of thousands of lucky Jane-Finch residents who, I'm sure, really enjoy the changing seasons in the park. The Black Creek Pioneer Village is closed in wintertime but you can sneak in the back way through the delivery entrance. Just don't tell them Hiker Mike sent you! Warn the dog people to keep 'em on a leash or you'll get that icy Toronto glare for letting Rover run loose. Hike with history at Black Creek.

54 Humber Arboretum

Hikers, if you're looking for a bit of nature in the city — gardens, forests, meadows and wetlands filled to the brim with butterflies, beavers, herons and kingfishers — then the Humber Arboretum is the hike for you. Not only can you hike on broad, paved pathways, good for strollers and wheelchairs, there are literally hundreds of forest and river trails, so you can custom fit your hike to include all of the above. The word *arboretum* is Latin for "tree museum."

Here, along the banks of the stately Humber, is a botanical garden; an ecological niche devoted to trees and woody plants; a beautiful forest chock full of maple, beech, ash, oak and hickory.

And it's in this forest and only in this forest that you'll find the Giant Horny Owl. So watch your back! Humber Arboretum is easy to get to. Take 401 west to Highway 27 north, to Humber College Boulevard, to Arboretum Boulevard. Go to the end and park in the lot. Give yourself three hours to hike end to end and back again.

KNOW YOUR DAMN TREES

I'd like to figure out a way to find out which tree is which. I don't know about the rest of you hikers out there on the trail of life, but I have a hell of a time remembering. What's the difference between a red and a white pine? A hemlock, beech or birch? Hey, how about the difference between the needles on the Austrian or jack pine? What does a hemlock look like, anyway? I'm flat-out embarrassed to tell you I just don't know. But I'm going to change all that. Let's play a game. Better yet, let's play an interactive multi-media game and we can call it (fanfare) "Know Your Damn Trees."

Now, here's how we play it. If you can identify one tree for absolutely sure and you can prove it, e-mail me the evidence to hikermike.com, the evidence being a picture of the tree and a small but witty description, and we'll put it up alongside the rest of the hard evidence and we'll build a "Know Your Damn Trees" web page. It's the only way we're ever going to learn the names of hundreds of big plants that grow across the length and breadth of this wonderfully bio-diverse ecological niche we call Toronto. The objective of the game is to be able to identify all the various trees, smugly or otherwise, before we're dead.

The Kortright Centre on Pine Valley Drive south of Major Mackenzie has little signs for all the trees in their hiking park — too many to memorize at once, but it'll get you started on knowing your damn trees. E-mail me at hikermike@hikermike.com and we'll send you Rupert the Malamute for a week! I'm just kidding. I wish I could send him; with the weather warming up, he's starting to stink. I swear if this dog isn't sitting on an iceberg, the smell coming off him would clear the whole cabin.

55 Claireville: Gone to the Dogs

I'm sad for the land, mad at the man, and sad for the land. Claireville Conservation Area in Brampton has so much going for it. Picture this! A few thousand acres of farmers' fields, agreement forests, lakes, rivers and wetland trails, complete with a huge reservoir, hawks and giant blue herons. Heavenly, huh? Now, run four major electric transmission lines sizzling and crackling with fallen snow, slashing right through the picnic area. And the boom and roar of jumbo jets taking off and landing at the Toronto Airport. And the new 407 ETR running along the southern boundary, competing for audio supremacy. Not great for a hiker guy with sensitive ears and an eye for beauty.

Now, on a more positive note! The peaceful Humber River flows right down the middle, and you can start your hike just off Highway 50 south of Highway 7 at the Etobicoke Field Study Centre. Go round back of the centre to find the trail, which will put you on a loop for two hours that you'll share with the dog people walking their canines. Points of interest on the trail: the Claireville Pony Ranch and a stunning view of the 407 ETR. Brings a tear to the old sherpa's eye.

Hikers, if you enjoy the juxtaposition of industry, noise and pollution with nature, peace and tranquillity, this is the hike for you. One thumb up and one thumb down. There is no joy in Claireville.

56 The Boyd, Woodbridge

The Boyd Conservation Area north of Woodbridge on Islington, 5 kilometres north of Highway 7, is a pristine beauty, hikers. It's truly a showplace for the Metro Conservation Authority — high pine forests and Humber River Valley — but what is truly remarkable is the well-marked hiking trail around the outside of the Boyd.

The trail starts just inside the main gates with big arrows pointing the way, taking you down to the Humber in the northeast corner of the park. And if you stay to the left after you cross the river, you'll come to the Humber Heritage Hiking Trail, which is part of the old (15th-century) native portage trail from Georgian Bay to Lake Ontario. This trail is so old, it takes the hike for you. But if you leave the path at the bottom of the park and keep to the fence, you'll come to an 80-year-old bridge. And if you jump the fence to go across the bridge, you're breaking the law, so think twice. But if you do —and I'm not recommending this move — you'll find yourself in the bottom half of the Boyd Conservation Authority, and that's nature at its wildest. It's hard to find a path except along the river. Up through the bush the path is very faint, so be really careful that you don't hurt any of the plant life.

It's a beautiful hike, but it's only an hour and a half tops. Families, seniors and wheelchairs stay on the main trails. Coureurs de bois and guerrillas, take a walk on the wild side and do the "big circle thing" around the park. The Boyd is four stars and a hiker's delight. Go for it, hikers, and be happy.

57 Kortright Centre: Hiker Heaven

I rose up last Sunday morning and was greeted by a bright blue sky; it looked like the perfect day for hiking. Got out my Secret Map and, gazing at the breakfast extravaganza before me, couldn't see one hiking entrée that made my mouth water. It was like going to a Pennsylvania Dutch smorgasbord without a two-day appetite. I was hiked out, hikers. The thought of hitting the trail just didn't appeal to me. But I had to do something, so I jumped in the car and started heading up Yonge Street, latte in hand, and my ever-faithful Rupert the Malamute in the back. I decided to go on a magical mystery hike, wherever the car took me. Next thing I knew

I was flying up the 400 when I saw a big green sign over the high-way that excited my blood. Major Mackenzie Drive. How can you go wrong on Major Mackenzie? It has adventure written all over it. There are hundreds of hikes everywhere you look, trails beckoning from just beyond the Major's soft shoulders. I turned west, drove 2 miles and found myself turning south on Pine Valley Drive, and there before me lay the locked-up gates of the Kortright Centre.

We hid our car in a farmer's lane and jumped the gate, only to bump into Kortright hiking guru Peter Attfield, who asked us what the heck we thought we were doing. I stammered something about Hiker Mike and CFRB, et cetera, and be darned if he didn't tell us to go on in and have a good hike.

A good hike? What an understatement! The Kortright Trail is a five-star 2½-hour hike, 15 kilometres of groomed nature trail.

It's got bridges and boardwalks over ravines and marshes; mature forest meadows; the Humber River Valley; streams and ponds and loads of wildlife — deer, racoons, herons, frogs and woodpeckers. There are even little signs naming all the trees.

A good trail to see a bit of everything is the 7K perimeter trail starting and ending at the visitor centre, with little You Are Here maps all along the trail, so you can't get lost. Heck, some of the trails are even wheelchair accessible. The Kortright Centre is open 10 am to 6 pm, 363 days a year, and getting there is easy.

You've got to hand it to enviro guys like Peter Attfield and Craig Mather from Metro Conservation, the way they put these hiking trails together. So, you coureurs de bois, test yourself in the open air of Mother Nature's sanctum sanctorum. Take a hike at Kortright. Cardiovascular fitness needs lots of hills to climb and pulse rates of 180 beats per minute. Your heart and lungs will scream for more. Hiking energizes you, makes you healthier, eat better, sleep better, feel happier.

58 Humber Trails Conservation Area

Pull out your Secret Map, hikers, and east of Nobleton by two concessions on King Road 11, south a half mile on Mill Street, you'll fall into Humber Trails Forest and Wildlife Conservation Area on King Creek in Nobleton. It's the perfect family hike along the bubbling and loquacious creek, where she marries with the tall, dark and handsome Humber River in a pasture-and-picnic-type setting (fried chicken and potato salad work really well here). Take your kids and dogs and have a picnic lunch with Mother Nature. And remember, it's always good to take your garbage with you — even organic waste such as orange and banana peels.

If you follow the grassy, mown path straight west to the end of the trail, you'll find a fireplace and a load of wood covered by a blue plastic tarp. The main trail ends here and you'll have to turn around. I can't figure this out. How can such a well-used path just stop? Granted, there are logs across the river, but no trails leading down to or away from them. You won't see any bikers here. It's just an old walking path up through the high bush, but down by King Creek it's a little mooshy, so wear your high-top boots to keep your feet dry.

Speaking of which, I got caught on the wrong side of the river — ran out of path because of erosion and it was too far to double back — so I took off the boots, hiked my pants up above my knees, and tap-danced through the shallows. See? I told you hiking's an adventure! Humber Trails — park your car under the old Humber Trails sign down by the River. Try it. You'll like it. Hiker Mike likes it and your family will too.

59. Humber Valley Heritage Trail

Hikers have to be the friendliest people in the world. The Urban Sherpas wanted to hike the Humber Valley Heritage Trail between Palgrave and Bolton so I put out a call for info and got two calls back. Hikers Dan O'Reilly and Bill Wilson both phoned and told us how to access the 15K trail, where to park our cars at either end, and what to look for on the trail. And here we are!

The Humber Valley Heritage Trail is a great four-hour hike through the Albion Hills, with some serious clambering, plenty of spots for swimming, and a great long-distance Smokey Mountain vista that will blow your mind. Just take your bug spray. And leave your dog at home; there are too many turnstiles and fence ladders. Head up Highway 50 to Columbus Way north of Bolton, and park in the Caledon Public Works yard opposite. You are now accessing the south end of the HVHT. Heading northwest on the trail, you'll hike through meadows and fields, low-down cedar groves, and upscale maple forests. The Heritage Trail intersects the Caledon Trailway, the Bruce Trail, and the fledgling Trans Canada Trail — great company for the new guy on the block.

The northern trailhead begins on the Humber Station Road north of the Old Church Road, where the Bruce and the Caledon Trailway (Cross Canada Trail) converge, and will eventually run south past Bolton all the way down the Humber to Lake Ontario. Imagine living in Albion Hills, like CFRB's Taylor "Hap" Parnaby, and walking to work in downtown Toronto. The trail building volunteers have put brand new steps and railings down the Humber Valley walls to the new bridges across the river. This trail is brilliantly marked with white blazes; it's a painstakingly well groomed pleasure path. The Humber Valley's terraced hillsides, down to cedar and up through maple bush, are stunningly beautiful anytime of year. Mountain forest panorama. *Aieey caramba, Cisco!*

Hikers living in the Greater Toronto area are so fortunate to have such diversity and choice in our trails — the Bruce, the Oak Ridges, the Ganaraska, and the river valleys of the Humber, the Credit, the Don, the Rouge and Duffins. But the jewel in the crown is none other than the Humber Valley Heritage Trail from Palgrave to Bolton. Congratulations to president Dan O'Reilly, Bill Wilson and everybody who works the trail. It's a joy to hike. Four hours from Humber Station to Columbia Way. For membership, call Gerry McNulty at 905-880-0772 to join. The Humber Valley Heritage Trail — winner of the 1999 Hiker Mike Golden Boot.

60 Glen Haffy: Source of the Humber

Heading up Highway 50 north, just before Albion Hills, you climb way up out of the Humber River Valley, and spreading out below you to the north and the west, you can watch the Caledon Hills stampeding headlong into the eastern flank of the Niagara Escarpment at Glen Haffy. It's a rainbow explosion of greens and reds and golds in autumn and just achingly beautiful to behold any time of year.

Glen Haffy, Scottish, I think, for "two landmasses colliding," lies at the junction of Airport Road and Highway 9. And if you follow the park road inside the gate to Lookout Point, you'll find the trailhead. The Red Trail and the Bruce join up to travel along the Escarpment valley carved by glacial meltwaters 14,000 years ago. Just keep your eyes on the trail, because the scenery will distract you, especially the pine forests, and you'll soon be lost. The white blazes of the Bruce will take you south (that's towards the sun, Bubba) down to the bottom of Glen Haffy Park to Maple Grove and Hilltop South. Just follow the road back north to your car.

Now, I was at Glen Haffy on a weekday. Even so, there was not a soul. Nobody. Glen Haffy needs families, kids, grandmas, pets and wheelchairs, hikers, so head on up Airport Road to Highway 9. Pay your $4 and put your boots to it. And take your picnic lunches and your fishing poles for use in the trout pond, which, by the way, is one of the sources of the Humber.

BUSHWACKER BORIS

Have I got news for you! Hiker extraordinaire Lorne Preston from Port Union sent me a copy of *Bushwacker, Ontario's Outdoor Adventure Magazine*. Twenty-four pages of power-packed hiking and canoeing information for outdoor people, great articles such as "Paddling the Saguine River," "Winery Hikes," "The Other Side of Algonquin," "Tough Trekking in Wakami," and the soon-to-be-published "Walking through Rosedale," by yours truly.

Bushwacker's published six times a year by the Bear Creek Company in Everett, Ontario, and besides the great articles, it's got letters to the editor, good local advertising, and a great classified section, and my favourite column — the list of upcoming hiking events. You can subscribe to *Bushwacker* for $15 a year. Call Boris at *Bushwacker*, 705-435-1211, or write to *Bushwacker*, RR 1, Everett, Ontario, L0M 1J0. *Bushwacker's* a great little hiking mag full of down-to-earth info for people with little exposure to the outdoors, like us city folk. So give yourself a treat, hikers. I know that *Bushwacker'll* inspire you.

Rouge River Hikes

What was the main river portage trail from Lake Ontario to Georgian Bay in the 17th century? The Rouge River Valley. River trails that run from Metro Toronto Zoo all the way down to the Rouge Marshes and Lake Ontario. Remember those great games of cowboys and Indians out in the forest when we were kids? That's what I felt like hiking the Rouge. I thought that Chingatchkook was gonna jump out and ambush me any second. I was so pumped!

TRAIL TALK

There are two kinds of hikers. The talkative kind and the quiet, contemplative kind. If you work alone during the week you'll probably want to yak your head off when you hit the trail, and that's okay. You've just got to find a kindred spirit who loves to talk as much as you. There are two things to remember.

1. Be sure to share the talk time 50-50 with your hiking buddy. It's no fun to listen to somebody for the entire hike without getting a chance to have your own say. Listen half the time, and talk half the time.

2. Try to stay away from the contemplative hikers who are out there communing quietly with nature.

Trail talk is a great way to blow off all your stress and troubles, but don't just bitch and complain, hikers. Let your sense of humour shine through, turn that frown upside down, Peewee, and smile. Do some bragging and make your stories interesting. Everybody wants to walk with a hiker whose cup is at least half full of the joy of life.

Rouge River Valley

There are so many different trails to hike in the Rouge River Valley that I try to get out there every season, and there's no better time than the fall. Rouge is French for red, and if you drive Meadowvale from the 401 to the Metro Zoo, you'll see what I mean. The fall colours will astonish you. Because the Rouge Valley is a well-protected south-facing sun pocket, the vegetation is Carolinian — what normally grows much further south — so not only do we see the changing colours of maple and oak but we're also treated to the more southerly hardwoods of hickory and chestnut with the more indigenous red and white pine thrown in with the beech and birch. It'll fill your eyes with Technicolor tears, and your heart with joy.

Instead of turning left off Meadowvale at the zoo entrance, turn right to Pearcy House and park in the lot. Pick up the Vista Trail south along the high ridge overlooking the Little Rouge where, for a thousand years, our First Nations people portaged from Lake Ontario to Lake Simcoe. Cross Twin Rivers Road and on the right you'll pick up the riverside trail along the flat valley floodplain, all the way south to Glen Rouge Campground, where most of you will take a break before heading back to Pearcy House.

But for you coureurs de bois who like it rough, keep on heading south under the Kingston Road down to Rouge Marshes and Lake Ontario to add another hour onto your journey. The Rouge is pure pleasure any time of year.

Bill Bryson's *A Walk in the Woods*

Hikers, if we were to play What's in My Backpack? right now, we'd find my Leatherman all-purpose tool, my Donabie Wannabe AM radio with Hiker Mike earplug, my digital phone for live reports from the trail, and my Speedo swimsuit for the halfway strip 'n' dip. We'd also find a darned good book. I inherited the love of books from my Ma, Mary Ann the Librarian, and right now the Hiker Mike Book of Choice is *A Walk in the Woods* by Bill Bryson. A 300-pound writer moves to a small town in New Hampshire and discovers a path going into the woods at the edge of town, and ends up hiking the 2,100 mile Appalachian Trail from Georgia to Maine. Hikers, this is an astonishingly funny book. I laughed till I cried. *A Walk in the Woods* is worth the extra weight in your backpack. It's not as heavy as a brick and infinitely more entertaining.

West Rouge: Top of the Zoo

Today we have a hike with plenty of choice. Your first choice is getting to the hike. From the 401 you can go north on either Meadowvale or Morningside to Old Finch Road. Find the parking lot beside the Rouge River and if you head south along the river, here's what you'll find: an excellent coureur de bois path, rugged enough to be interesting, yet predictable enough not to get you lost.

Hike #1: If you follow the path along the east bank south, you'll have the Metro Zoo on your left and the pristine Rouge River on your right. This is a cliffside path at times that'll take you so high above the river you'll get vertigo. Lots of big erosion, so stay well back from the edge, especially in the springtime. And on your left through the zoo fence, you'll see dozens of huge, hairy muskox and camels and all sorts of foreign animals staring back at you. The only problem, hikers, is that you run out of path in about 45 minutes, because the zoo fence comes down to meet the river and, in order to continue, you've got to cross the zoo property through the lion area.

Now, I know guerrilla hikers go where they're not supposed to, but I've got to draw the line here. Wouldn't it be an adventure if you bumped into a pride of lions having a drink down at the old watering hole? That'd get your big fat bum moving, wouldn't it? So it's a 90-minute hike all round, with plenty of ups and downs to get your cardiovascular going boom, boom.

Now *Hike #2*: I'm an inquisitive guy. I always want to know where the path goes, so when I got back to the parking lot, I kept going under the Finch Avenue Bridge, heading north this time, and I found a fallen tree that crossed the river, so Rupert and I tightroped it and found ourselves on a huge path heading up the west side of the Rouge.

This is a great two-hour hike that loops back around on itself. So you get two hikes for the price of one. Meadowvale or Morningside to Old Finch Road? Take your pick, park the car and hike till you knees seize.

Rouge Trailblazer

It's seldom I get so excited about finding a hike that I start thinking in terms of the Golden Boot Award for Best Guerrilla Hike so early in the year. But I feel like Archimedes in the bathtub, discovering water displacement and screaming Eureka! I have found it! And hikers, I've found it!

Head out the 401 east to Morningside, north to Old Finch Road, turn right, head east until you come down into the Rouge Valley past the housing development, cross the steel bridge and pull into the parking lot. Instead of heading south along the established path into zoo country, cross under the steel bridge and head north up the east side of the river. The going gets a little rough right off the top, as the path soon degenerates into an animal trail, and because of the heavy erosion, you've got to scramble over and under fallen trees that have come down to meet the river.

Watch your footing because this path is very tricky and dangerous, and soon you'll find yourself bushwhacking down an old railway bed arcing into the forest thick with dense undergrowth. The going gets tough before it gets easier, but the trick is to stick to the river until you come upon a 150-foot cliff wall up whose slippery flanks you must climb. But once you reach the top, and that takes some doing, hikers, you'll come upon an old trail hundreds of feet above the Rouge, horseshoeing willy-nilly below you, and a huge bowl of a ridge walk heading north upriver. This is a long-forgotten and disused trail worthy of a guerrilla hiker armed with his topographical map and heavy boots.

Back in the bush about 50 to 60 feet from the ridge you come across an ATV trail that will take you north to an old east-west railway line running parallel to the new railroad. Head west across Sewells Street on the old railway bridge that they use in the IKEA commercials, and back down into the Rouge River Valley, and take the path south along the east side of the Rouge. When you come back to the steel bridge on Sewells, you've got a choice. You can be a sissy and walk the Old Finch back to your car, or you can cross the Frank Barber Bridge and head into the bush on the other side of the river and see if you can make the difficult ascent up another 150-foot cliff then tumble down the other side into the parking lot. This is a great 2½-hour guerrilla hike only for those in the best of shape.

Back in the parking lot, we met an old New Zealander named Ken Hay who comes down to the river every day to feed the birds. The Rouge at the Old Finch Bridge reminds him of his youth in New Zealand. It's that beautiful. How can such an amazing piece of nature be 20 minutes from downtown Toronto?

64 Reesor Road to Pearcy

W e're going to follow the Rouge south from the corner of Reeser Road and Steeles, parking on the southeast corner. Follow the widest, most-used path south through the park as close to the west side of the river all the way down to the railway bridge, crossing underneath, and continue down until it turns into an animal path. Pass through a red pine forest and that spills you out onto a high ridge of the Rouge. Follow it south.

The early spring is the best time for exploring. The snow's not so bad for hiking; it's crunchy underfoot. And also, if you're going off the beaten trail into the depths of the forest, you can always find your way out by following your footsteps from whence you came. Follow the animal trails through the sumac-loaded floodplain. When you come across an east-west trail that takes you down to the river to the foundations of an old bridge, that's where you join up with the main trail heading south. This

is a hike where the main trail often keeps disappearing because of washouts and erosion. Follow the big path on the east side of the river once you cross Meadowvale, cross the old steel bridge, get on the east side and head south. It's as wide as a highway all the way down to the Metro Zoo.

Just to the south of Meadowvale there's a wonderful vantage point — a sun-pocket ridge looking over the Rouge Valley as the river winds its way into the zoo — where some-one has hewn a large maple bench well-placed to take in the view some 150 feet off the water. From the bench you'll find a path climbs the valley wall with the help of some built-in steps and a nice railing, and from there, the world's your oyster. Off to the left you'll see the Beare Road landfill site at the zoo, and the road leading to the Pearcy House, and the Vista and Orchard Trails that can take you all the way down the river to the Rouge Campgrounds and Lake Ontario.

Today we chose to walk east past Pearcy House and out to Meadowvale, past the entrance to the zoo, then back north on Meadowvale to Reesor Road and our car. So half the hike was heavy slogging along the river and the other half was a road boot back to the Meadowvale steel bridge, then following our foot-prints back through the bush to the car. Next time it'll be a two-car hike from Reeser Road to the Campgrounds down at Highway 2 and Kingston Road.

AGAINST THE WIND

Late winter, early spring is the worst time to go hiking in the woods because of the ice, the snow and the flooding, so my best advice to you hikers is to stay on the backroads. Hiking around a whole country concession will only take you a couple of hours. Let me give you a helpful hiking hint before you go. Always check the wind direction and hike into it as you begin. So when it's time to turn around and head for home, you'll have the wind and weather at your back when you're all tuckered out and you need a little boost. I found this out the hard way, swimming home against the current.

CHAPTER
10

Megacity Fringe Hikes

ONLY U CAN PREVENT

FLA DIVISION

65 Bronte Creek, Oakville

Last Sunday morning, I discovered Bronte Creek Provincial Park, just off the QEW in Burlington and Oakville. Such a variety of trails for moms, dads, kids and grandparents, people in wheelchairs, all hiking on the river, bush and farmland trails, all well marked and well worn, and right in the middle, a magic mountain with a vista looking over the golden Escarpment to the west, Lake Ontario to the south and Bronte River Valley and Toronto to the east.

Do you know what all those guys at Stelco, Ford, Dofasco and Shell do on the weekends? They take their kids to Bronte Creek to play in the Children's Farm, then take their wives on a hike for an hour.

For you coureurs de bois who like your hiking a little more primitive: The east side of the creek off Highway 25 has not been developed and is a rigorous two-hour attack on the path less travelled. Bronte Creek Provincial Park is 30 minutes from Yonge and Front. Take the QEW to Burloak Drive north. Good hiking in all seasons.

66 Sawmill Creek, Mississauga

Early last Saturday morning I loaded up on coffee black and headed out the Gardiner West to Mississauga Road just north of Dundas, and parked at the Springbank Visual Arts Centre, crossed the road, and found myself on the Sawmill Creek Trail in the wilds of Erin Mills.

Sawmill Creek sits in a sun pocket sheltered by hills on either side, and as you hike north along the water, you find yourself in a very Southern Carolinian forest of hickory, walnut and beech trees. But after a half hour or so the path keeps trying to dump you into every kind of housing development known to man.

Fight the confusion, hikers! As they say in Key West, "Keep on keepin' on, baby." As long as you're on the creek, it's heaven. Your objective, should you decide to accept it, is to find your way to Burnhamthorpe and Glen Erin Drive, and just behind the Ignatius Loyola School you'll find a sign for the Glen Erin Trail, which will take you south to make a loop back to the bottom of Sawmill Creek — an hour and a half tops. The big feature of the Sawmill Creek is the trail itself. It's flat and wide and mostly paved, so it's great for families, kids, seniors and wheelchairs. I never realized how beautifully designed Mississauga and Erin Mills are, with greenbelt paths and parkways linking neighbourhood schools, churches and shops. You can walk everywhere, and that's why I'm moving my family here.

For you coureurs du bois out there, check out the Credit Valley Footpath behind the Springbank Visual Arts Centre (3057 Mississauga Road). Folks tell me you can walk from Lake Ontario to the 403.

Eden Mills to Guelph on the Eramosa River

I am curious yellow. I've always hiked down trails and over fences to find out what's through the bush, or round the next bend, and I'm glad I did last Sunday when the Urban Sherpas Rolling Review descended on the sleepy little village of Eden Mills, just south of Highway 7, nestled on the Eramosa River between Rockwood and Guelph. I grew up in this neck of the woods and I hiked the river valley as a kid, over 40 years ago, so I knew there was lots more to discover. And boy, did we discover! There's a big mowed snowmobile and cross-country ski trail that loops east along the river towards Rockwood at Barden and York Street, which also runs behind the houses on Main Street, so you can peek in and watch the natives at play in their backyards.

But the real fun begins at the west end of Barden Street at

Wellington Road 29. There we found the old Guelph Trail along the river — 5 beautiful miles through birch pasture and cedar hollow, up onto the ridge, and miles of blue-ridged mountain vista all the way to the Tim Hortons on Victoria Street in downtown Guelph. The trail is well marked with red blazes along Lilac Lane, featuring a sheer limestone cliff looming over the river opposite the Guelph Reformatory. Only three hours roundtrip, and the Guelph Trail guys and girls ask only that you don't light fires, hike only along the marked trail, and take your litter with you. Try a two-car hike from Eden Mills, home of the Eden Mills Writers Festival, to Guelph, home of the Guelph Jazz Festival.

Eden Mills is a cool summer hike through the sleepiest of villages, which reminds me to tell you about the Country Spirit Bed and Breakfast in Eden Mills. Jane Isbrucker will show you all the trails. Call her at Country Spirit, 1-519-856-9879, for a weekend of hiking and riverside lovemaking away from the city. So hikers, please, get curious, see where it all leads, and hike the Guelph Trail in Eden Mills.

68 Heart Lake, Brampton

Recently, Hiker Mike and the Urban Sherpas hiked the Heart Lake Conservation area at 410 and Highway 7, just north of Brampton. Heart Lake has an 8K nature trail that got us all het up, and so after the hike, we hit the beach to work on our tans and our backstroke in Heart Lake's cool, crystal waters.

Every spring, Heart Lake is stocked with rainbow trout for the Annual Fishing Derby, and you can try to take them home for dinner, or you can take the fixings with you for a barbecue and picnic right there. Heck! You can even rent a paddleboat for fishing or just messing around. But one thing to remember, hikers. Heart Lake is unsupervised, with no lifeguards on duty. So keep an eagle eye on your kids.

Heart Lake's a beauty. Just 20 minutes west of Toronto at 410 and 7.

Mulmer Mansfield Ski Hikes

I have skis. I've skied my whole life but I've had enough of it. I don't feel a big thrill getting up on the boards anymore. The wild and wacky downhill, the long and endless cross-country. Folks are forever saying to me, "Hiker Mike, why don't you come skiing with us. Let's go ski the Caledons. Let's go up to Mansfield." Well, now I've got a good reason for going, because when they go up to ski at Mansfield, I head down the road toward the Dufferin Forest and the Road Allowance hiking trails.

And this all came about because of a lovely lady from Andrew's Scenic Acres out Milton way named Julie Underwood who once wondered out loud on my answering machine why I hadn't been up north of Highway 89 to hike Mulmur Township. Julie's one of these hikers who's been everywhere, and the vision of a leafy path disappearing into the woods with a Keep Out sign in front of it excites Julie no end! Bruce Trail blazes and Oak Ridges Trail markings do nothing for Ms Underwood. She's got the topographical maps for all Ontario and she's been blazing her own trails for many years. Julie gave me directions to her secret hikes in the Mansfield area (which I'm not going to share with you) and she also sent me two books by Harvey Currell of *Toronto Telegram* fame. Mr. Currell probably knew Ontario better than any other human because in the '50s and '60s he drove and hiked thousands of miles to gather material for his weekly town and country trips column.

Harvey has hiked Beausoleil Island in Georgian Bay, the Beaver River Valley, Elora, West Montrose and Belfountain, to name but a few, and now Harvey's disciple Julie Underwood has opened a whole new area to hike — the Mulmur Township in Dufferin County, including the Mansfield Hike and the Bruce Trail section of the Pine River.

Come up the Airport Road, past 89 to the Mansfield Ski Centre, turn left and continue to the end of the road and where it T-bones at the Mulmur 20 Sideroad. You'll find a big blue sign:

Welcome to the Huronia Snowmobile Southern Zone. Ride. Respect. Enjoy.

So this is where the hike begins, in full view of the Mansfield ski trails directly to our rear. We'll be heading north through big pine forest. Lots of birds, beautiful brown-red clay and a government-owned road allowance we're allowed to walk through. These roads divide private properties, but we, the citizens, own the thoroughfare.

The road allowance is quite wide and easily accessible, but we're doing a serious cardio workout here. Lots of Keep Out signs on either side of the road. Don't trespass. This is a combination forest walk and road hike, so you can use this all year round. In the winter the snowmobiles will provide you with a good firm track for walking, and then of course the concession roads are plowed, so you've got the best of both. We passed into the gigantic Dufferin Agreement Forest on the left, full of old-growth white pines, and a trail leading up out of the cedar river valley into a high hardwood forest. It took us approximately 45 minutes to circle the forest, which looped us back onto the snowmobile track taking us south via the road allowance, back to our car on the 20 Sideroad. Roundtrip time totals about 1½ hours.

To make it a more substantial hike, why not park in the Mansfield Ski Centre's parking lot, which is a good 25 minutes down the road. This will add an hour to your hike and make it worthwhile to travel all the way from Toronto. You could also combine the morning hike with lunch back at the ski centre, and an adventurous 3½-hour hike on the Bruce Trail down the Pine River Road not far from here to the west. Just remember Hiker Mike's old maxim, "Go where they ain't." Spring, summer and fall are the best times for Mansfield hikes, in and around the ski areas of Dufferin County.

We did get lost once north of the Dufferin Forest. I get hopelessly lost all the time. Once I'm in the forest on the trail, I get into the hiking groove, my mind slips out the side door, and those blasted trail blazes disappear on me. I must pay more attention. I saw a gentleman farmer out standing in his field and shouted at him, asking permission to come aboard, which means crossing onto his property. I could see by the way his face lit up that

he appreciated the gesture. His name was Walter Drake and he gave us the great idea for hiking the Pine River Provincial Fishing Park, which lies between the little village of Terra Nova and Hornings Mills just a few miles to the west of Mansfield. The Bruce Trail crosses the River Road several times, so you can find it easily.

The River Road from Terra Nova to Hornings Mills, north of Shelbourne, is quite famous, as Toronto media people have begun moving there: Dini Petty, Andy Barrie, and my producer-engineer at CFRB, Bob Lehman. Bob has been raving about the Pine River Bruce Trail, just steps from his house on the River Road, as he walks his golden retrievers there every day, so he knows the trail pretty well. This is God's country, hikers. Take the day, or weekend, to hike Mulmur in the Dufferin County. Or just move there, like Bob.

Seaton Trail at Green River Duffins Creek

We're hiking the Seaton Trail at Green River, along the West Duffins Creek, in Pickering. Everybody knows where the Rouge River is, right? At the Zoo. Well, this is one major river valley to the east of the Rouge, and boy, oh boy, is this guerrilla hiking at its best. Three times I've tried this hike and failed twice. Christmas Day I started up at the top of Highway 7 at the little town of Green River, and got driven back by icy trails. Boxing Day I ran out of trail and dead-ended when the trail disappeared at a giant erosion washout by Clarke's Hollow. So this time, I'm starting at the bottom of the hike at Brock Road and Finch. I hid my car behind the billboard at the southeast corner and I'm not leaving here till I get it right.

A little history of the Seaton Trail on Duffins Creek, whose source can be found near the Hamlet of Goodwood. Five hundred years ago the Duffins was a whitewater trailway, 35K to Lake Ontario, used by our early Ojibwa brothers. The fast-running green river was named for the Irish trapper Duffin, a gnarly old man who built his cabin at its mouth in 1780, then quickly vanished; the locals suspected foul play. The lush river valley was farmed in the 1800s, but many villages and mills have since disappeared, leaving only the crossroads of Green River in the north on Highway 7, Whitevale and Clarke's Hollow around Taunton Road, and Old Pickering Village down Lake Ontario way at Kingston Road. There was a time, not so long ago, when the authorities had earmarked the Duffins Valley for the new Pickering Airport, but since the public outcry cancelled the project, the Duffins has slipped back into its sleepy and serene natural state. The Seaton Trail runs some 10K up the Duffins' flanks through a most pleasant refuge of wooded slopes and floodplain meadows, while whitewater river rapids challenge even the most experienced canoeists in the springtime.

Megacity Fringe Hikes

You may access the Seaton Trail at Highway 7, some 5 miles east of Markham at Green River, or take the Brock Road exit north from the 401, then the first left north of Finch, or head up Whites Road north from the 401 to Forest Trail Road down into Clarke's Hollow. The trail is marked with yellow rings and is easy to follow once you're on it.

The Duffins is going to test your hiking ability. Best you follow the Seaton up the east side of the Duffins; God knows it's tough enough. But if you want to go guerrilla, take the west side of the creek — you could get lost, or cold and wet in the river, or maybe even injured. Man, you're walking on the wild side. There's little or no path because of the huge cave-ins. Whole hillsides have come down to the river through erosion, and you gotta scramble. The river really is green and it's noisy and it shouts up at you. Lots of rapids. The trail is an even darker green and tight in the conifers, and the cedar ladies sneak up and give you a little snow kiss for your trouble, but the western path is so treacherous, you could end up knee-deep in the icy rapids, like Tracker Dave. It was a long way back to the car that day, eh, Tracker?

It's 2½ hours up to Clarke's Hollow, but it's an easy 2-hour cakewalk back to your car down the Seaton Trail on the other side. Wouldn't you know it, the Seaton Trail was there all along. I had been killing myself on the wrong side of the river. I can be such a maroon sometimes.

Merry Little Breezes
Ajax–Pickering

In high summer, we Megacitizens sometimes dwell in Dante's Seventh Circle. Damnably hot. Even when we seek relief from the heat, it's tough to find the cool and welcoming Merry Little Breezes. Oh, sure, you say. Go on down to Harbourfront, or Ontario Place or Sunnyside. But maybe you're a private person and you like to hike with

Mother Nature and not with a half million hot and testy people. So what's a body to do? I'll tell you, hikers. Go where they're not.

Hike the Ajax–Pickering Waterfront Trail from the nuclear station through Montgomery Park, to Rotary Park and up to Lion's Point, and all the way east to Shoal Point Road. There's an asphalt trail for miles, and beach and ridge trails intertwining it — so cool, baby, breezes for days and nice people to boot. Take 401 east to Harwood south, matey. Continue on till your feet get wet in good old Lake Ontario. Back up a bit and you're standing on the boardwalk. Walk the planks for an hour or two and cool yourself off.

P.S. Did you know that those two flying, half-nude fairies in Botticelli's "Rising of Venus" are none other than the Merry Little Breezes and they're called the Zephyrs?

72 Ganaraska

A while ago I took a hike with Peter Heinz, then Hike Ontario president, and his hardy band of directors, after their annual meeting. Hiker Mike led the group down the Don River through the Sauriol Reserve, and it only took me about 20 minutes to get everyone totally lost! You see, we dead-ended up a canyon and ran out of trail. And that gave us plenty of time to get to know each other while we searched for the path back to the parking lot.

One of the guys, David Francis, new Hike Ontario president, is also the president of the Ganaraska Trail Association. The trail extends from Port Hope on Lake Ontario all the way to Glen Huron, nestled in the Niagara Escarpment just south of the Blue Mountains. David told me about the central wilderness section of the Ganaraska, running 65K through Precambrian Shield over rugged terrain from Moore Falls to Sedowa. You need a guidebook, a map and a compass to hike the Ganaraska. It's one tough hike. So, if you live up by Barrie and Midland down to Peterborough and Port Hope, why not join the Ganaraska Club? Call President David Francis at 905-729-4545 and become a member.

Ganaraska Wilderness Trail

I was standing on top of Scrabble Mountain looking at the grave of Aldie Lecroix, who was born in 1893 and died in 1966; there were crossed snowshoes on the front of his tombstone. We were up on the Ganaraska Wilderness Trail just north of Devil's Lake and Moore Falls off Highway 35 south of Miner's Bay, heading 13 kilometres into the bush toward Petticoat Junction, where we were going to have some lunch, a swim and a snooze.

We planned on four hours to get to Petticoat and the bush was spectacular, but the trail was completely minimal. Oh, yes! There were times when the trail was as wide as a logging road, but for the most part the trail was non-existent.

The white blazes on the trees were so hard to follow that we would stand with our hand on one of the blazed trees and send hikers on ahead to find the next. This makes for very difficult hiking. Remember, we're criss-crossing landmasses here. It's Precambrian, all granite, pink and wonderful, and if your attention wanders for a moment you can become hopelessly lost. The Ganaraska Trail Association advises all hikers to take a map and a compass, and let someone know what section you're hiking and when you expect to finish.

Once we reached the top of Scrabble Mountain and had our lunch, we decided we'd gone far enough and Petticoat Junction would have to wait for the next hike, and so we turned around and headed for home. It was a cakewalk to get back because old faithful Malamute Rupert the Wonder Dog took the lead and made a beeline through the bush, never letting us out of his sight until we were back at the car, some 10K away. The Urban Sherpas loved the arduous irregularities of the trail. We adored the 360-degree view from the top of Scrabble Mountain, but could you please blaze the trail a little better, Mr. Ganaraska, so we don't have to spend more time looking for the trail than actually hiking it?

The Ganaraska Wilderness Trail: a five-star boot. If it weren't for the bears, the wolves and the deer who hike the trail regularly, we poor humans would never have been able to follow it. Take 401 to Highway 35 north past Lindsay to Moore Falls and Black Lake Road. Turn left, park your car and hike to your heart's desire. To be continued...

Ganaraska Wilderness Trail, May 1, 1999

Because I raised such a ruckus about the scarcity of trail markings, hike leader Peter Verbeek invited me along on the Springtime Hike, May 1, 1999, some eight months later, and here is that report.

May 1, 1999, was the annual Ganaraska Hike, through almost 20K of some of the most spectacular and arduous Haliburton Highlands topography, up Highway 35 north of Moore's Falls. The hike was rough, tough and relentless, on top of the fact that the blackflies were in full bloom, and to further complicate the six-hour marathon, a cross-section of more than 50 hikers with varying degrees of hiking skill showed up in Moore's Falls at 9 am. That's right. Fifty-odd hikers, from late teens to mid-70s, some of whom were the best hikers I have seen this side of the Himalaya, and some day players who were there for a walk in the park, without their requisite 3 litres of water, if you catch my drift (read inexperienced).

Here's how you get 50 hikers through 20K of Precambrian jungle. First you start with the Lead Hiker — a kind of rabbit to set the pace — and off go the Alpha Hikers through the bush. Don't try to keep up with those guys and gals. They're very competitive and resentful of any other hiker replacing them in their line position.

Then after the gamesters, come the experienced hikers in the middle who carry their 3 litres of water and make a joyful day of it. Then at the back of the pack is a mixed bag of beginners and hiking wounded who may find that they're in just a little over their head. At the extreme back of the pack is the Sweep — an experienced cheerleader hiker who keeps everyone going with jokes and stories, and a sympathetic ear for the complaints coming from the sore and weary who are about to give up. And spanning the entire half mile range of hikers is the Trail Boss — Peter Verbeek — who runs the show, whistling lunch stops and pee breaks, and making sure the head count is the same from beginning to end.

We were hiking a 20K loop through wicked underbrush, over Precambrian mountain and Shield, descending countless times to water valleys of lakes and rivers, tight-roping across beaver dams, and mud swamps, only to climb straight back up to the top of the rockface, and begin all over again. We stopped three or four times in six hours for 15 minutes, sitting down under a tree to try getting out of a blazing springtime sun in a cloudless sky. But there were no leaves on the trees, so shelter was scarce. Very hot and glary and bright. Headache country, hikers.

The front third of the pack moved effortlessly through the bush, keeping a steady aggressive pace and getting back to their cars a good half hour before the rest started to arrive. Peter had stressed to me on many an occasion that only the most experienced hikers would enjoy this Ganaraska Wilderness boot, and now I understand completely. I started to doubt my own abilities in the last endless hour of the trek, and it was a very tired and sore Hiker Mike who, after the long trek was over, moaned in pain quietly to himself all the way back to Toronto where Mrs. Mike administered to his every need with chicken soup and Irish stew and a half a case of Perrier (pretty multicultural repast, eh?).

And so it all worked out, thanks to hike leader Peter Verbeek, who worked his heiny off; not only getting all 50 of us through, but also taking care of the non-glamorous side of hiking — trail grooming and tree blazing. What a guy! Thanks for the day, Verbeek, you're a mench. For more info on the Ganaraska Wilderness Trail, write Ganaraska Hiking Association, Ganaraska Trail, Box 693, Orillia, Ontario, L3V 6K7, or email ck281@torfree.net

Hikers, you are never to attempt the Ganaraska Wilderness Trail without bug repellent, a protective hat, 3 litres of water, a lunch, a map and a compass. If you do, you're a doughhead.

URBAN MYTH #1: LOCAL HONEY

There's an urban myth or an old wive's tale, I don't know which, but it goes something like this: "Eat the honey from your local area and your allergies will ease up and eventually disappear." Now I'm one of those guys whose eyes go nuts in the spring with all that itching and watering when the pollen starts to fly; some days I'd gladly rip these affected orbs from their sockets and throw them into the Duffins Creek if I could, the itching is so bad.

I do like to sneeze once or twice. It's good to clear your brain and sinuses, but it's no help even carrying a box of Kleenex with me, the way I sneeze and spray continuously in the early spring. All I want to do is move to Arizona. I mentioned this to the Honey Man out Bruce Trail way, up north of Milton, and he told me to eat more of his honey to stop the allergies. I thought it was a marketing ploy to get me to buy the extra-large barrel, but I took him at his word, and let me tell you, the honey has made a difference.

The logic of it is as follows: The bees bring home all the various pollens from the local flowers and plants, and put it into the honey, so we start to build up an immunity to that which makes us sneeze and itch, and over time we become inoculated to our local vegetation — kind of a welcome to Mother Nature's private club, secret handshake and all. Makes sense, doesn't it? Anybody out there got proof for or against this theory? E-mail me at hikermike@hikermike.com and give me the goods and I'll send you Rupert the Malamute for the week as a prize.

 Megacity Fringe Hikes

Guerrilla Hikes

The whole idea of guerrilla hiking — hiking in Keep Out areas, disobeying No Trespassing signs, working from topographical maps and charting your own course — came from my old pal Red-Headed Kenny. We grew up in Kitchener together. Not only was he one hell of an athlete, Kenny was also a poacher. Armed with maps of the area, fishing line and a little case of plastic hooks in his pocket, Kenny'd stuff a couple of dew worms in his cheeks and crawl on his belly under gates and fences in search of private trout streams and ponds.

Needless to say, I'm a lot older these days and I don't recommend anybody trespassing on private property, but I have a heck of a time restraining myself when I see a beautiful trail disappearing into the woods with a Keep Out sign in front of it. So I satisfy this urge by sneaking into abandoned Conservation lands or following a river valley like the Humber to its source. We Mega-citizens own this property, but if anything happens to us while hiking the Metro lands, we are liable. A word to the wise.

That having been said, Hiker Mike's recommended guerrilla hikes are: The Etobicoke Creek from Eglinton to the Lake, Cold Creek Conservation Area up Bolton way, Palgrave Forest north of Albion Hills, St. George's in Oak Ridges, and Claremont in north Pickering. These are closed-down areas that should be trail-blazed and new paths made. They're too beautiful to be left untended. So, go down to the Mountain Equipment Co-op and pick up the topo maps for the Toronto area. Guerrilla hiking will keep your sense of adventure alive, and you won't be hurting anybody as long as you're careful. Clear the old trails as you go and stuff any garbage in your backpack. Leave every place better for your having been there. The four Energy, Mines and Resources maps you'll need are #30M11, Toronto; #30M12, Brampton; #30M13, Bolton; and #30M14, Markham.

Caveat Emptor, hikers. We're not advising you to hike restricted areas, we're only telling you where we've hiked and what we've seen. Proceed at your own risk.

Palgrave Forest: The Forgotten Trail

There's something dark and brooding about Palgrave Forest. I feel like Heathcliff on the moors. Now I suppose the looming grey-granite clouds and the howling wind and freezing late-autumn rain didn't help the mood, but in spite of all that, the hike through Palgrave Forest just north of Bolton was downright exhilarating.

Up Highway 50 north of Palgrave Village, on the left, sits a big old-fashioned brown and yellow Metro Conservation sign that says The Kelley Tract of the Palgrave Forest. Enter Palgrave Forest through the fence heading west and find yourself in a giant meadow surrounded by cedar and pine monsters — reds and whites planted in the '40s to stem the Caledon's topsoil erosion. You see, the top of the Palgrave Hills were blown away by wind and rain when Caledon loggers cleared this section hundreds of years ago for farming. But since the heavy replanting of the '40s, part of a make-work war effort, a walk through this pine forest a half century later is a Strauss waltz through the Garden of Eden, a forest primeval, rife with overgrown and untended vegetation. At the trailhead you'll notice two tin-roofed outhouses sitting under an ancient Trailway sign — three trails, two keybowles, no waiting. A beginner 4K, an intermediate 4K — just who the hell are you intermediate hikers, anyway? — and the expert 9K Red Trail, which travels the circumference of the forest.

Up the Red Trail and into the forest I go. You've got to remember, nobody hikes the Palgrave Forest, because it's the poor sister to the Albion Hills Conservation Area just south of here and more in favour with Torontonians, so Palgrave is truly the path less travelled. Remember "Go where they ain't," hikers? I saw only one hiker's footprints on the trail that day, and the great Bruce Trail, which cuts through Palgrave on the diagonal, had absolutely no footprints to call her own. Sacrilege!

Along the southern boundary, the trail takes you past the foot of a hill, on top of which sits a triple-trunked maple crowning its crest. Jump off the trail and climb to the maple and then behold ye Mother Nature's Humber Valley stretching majestically south to Bolton. Palgrave is a jewel in the Caledon crown but it is not open to the public, so hike well at your own peril, guerrillas. Go ye therefore, hikers, and hike ye all green spaces, trailblazing them in the name of Mother Nature, Hiker Mike and the one lone Palgrave Forest hiker whose footprints we saw that day.

14 Cold Creek

Never thought I'd find Cold Creek, and when I did, the grounds reminded me of Miss Haversham's of *Great Expectations.* The gatehouse of the conservation area was covered in cobwebs, and peeling paint. And it was Keep Out closed to boot. Time for guerrilla tactics. I jumped the fence, and immediately bumped into an old hiker named Jim who told me there was a horse path around the whole 750 acres of Cold Creek. "Go through the pine forest down past a few lakes, through the old farm, and in behind the abandoned visitors centre you'll come across an old trail down to the black spruce bog," said Jim.

"Okay," said I.

You know, 10,000 years ago, the Wisconsin Glacier melted and made this whole area a shallow lake, and in Cold Creek a sphagnum peat-moss bog was formed, and since it was so acidic in nature, black spruce and Labrador tea began to grow there. Right through the middle of this bog runs a wooden walkway — must be a quarter to a half mile long — and under the walk-way is the Coooooold Creek. And I oughta know, hikers. It was so inviting, I stripped off my hiking gear and took the plunge. April 22nd — my first swim of '98. C-c-c-c-c-cold! Ooo-eeee-man! They must have run out of money because Cold Creek is closed, but they don't mind hikers going in. Just remember — you're liable — so be on your best behaviour. Cold Creek is a guerrilla hiker's dream. Five-star. Take Highway 50 north to Bolton Bridge, turn right to Nobleton, then north on the 11th Concession, past Glen Cedar Conference Centre. It's on your right about 2 miles. Takes 2½ hours around the park. Be there or be a big sissy.

75 Etobicoke Creek

Now I know it's a little wet to try the Mimico Creek on for size right now, so I'm only flirting with it. I'm at the Humber Bay Park on Lake Ontario at the bottom of the Mimico. You can walk the park itself for an hour then follow the shore over to Palace Pier and Sunnyside along the Boardwalk if you need some extra distance. But I swear, as soon as it gets drier in the spring, the flirting's over and the affair begins with the Mimico and the Etobicoke Creeks.

The Etobicoke Creek. I look at it in my Rand McNally and it smiles back at me. Part of an ancient limestone sea 450 million years old. It runs all the way from Eglinton Avenue and Rakely in the north, down to Lake Ontario and Marie Curtis Park on the Lakeshore. So I called up a few of my Urban Sherpa buddies and we hit the trail. We left one car on Rakely south of Eglinton and headed south along the creek — a trail less travelled — until we came out from under the Rathburn Bridge and into the Markland Wood Country Club.

"Get out of here! You're on a private course!" Golf balls buzzing over our heads. *Zzzzt! Zzzzt!* But we decided to stay right next to the creek, be polite to everyone, and keep moving south at all costs. Then the manager wheeled up to us in his golf cart, and it looked like the end of the trail for us.

"I'm Hiker Mike from CFRB," says I, "We're hiking the Etobicoke Creek this morning. I'm sorry we're trespassing."

"Oh, that's okay," he said. "Go ahead. I listen to CFRB all the time."

South of Bloor we hit an industrial park. So as we were heading down South Creek Road toward Dundas, we heard a voice say, "You wouldn't be Hiker Mike, would you? I just heard you on the radio!" And local David Ibonie proceeded to show us the path south of Dundas.

Etobicoke Creek is a great four-hour obstacle course. Plan on getting wet. But it's all worthwhile south of the QEW because the path turns into a paved bicycle trail and you're home free. The Creek is a rest stop on the migratory trail to hundreds of species of fish and birds including big blue herons and hawks. It's Carolinian vegetation rife with huge hemlock and pine. Take lots of food and water. This hike's a knockout, hikers.

Still to come? The Mimico Creek. Definitely Volume 2...

16 St. George's Conservation Area

It's so seldom I'm disappointed when I go on a hike these days. All I need, after all, is some semblance of a path with a star to steer her by...know what I mean? So it's with some reluctance that I report to you on the St. George Conservation Area opposite Lake Wilcox and Sunset beach up in Oak Ridges just to the northeast of Richmond Hill. At best, it's a guerrilla hike, because you have to hop the fence to get in, and at worst, it's just another Metro Conservation area closed down due to lack of funds.

St. George has been left to return to Mother Nature's clutches — no trail maintenance — bridges and railings rotting away, trail markers faded to disappearing. So common sense and keen directional skills are a must while hiking. But hang in there, hikers, because there are hundreds of hectares of lake, forest, meadow, and thousands of birds. The entrance to St. George is on the Bethesda Sideroad, but they discourage you from using it. Not Open to the Public signs everywhere, but I didn't see any No Hiker signs, so just keep your head down, guerrillas and hit the bush quick once inside. Or you can park opposite Sunset Beach on Bayview and combine the St. George hike with a swim and a hike around Lake Wilcox. Add 45 minutes. And though you have to search around for a path at the west end, it's a 2½-hour adventure you won't soon forget.

Some years ago, hikers, I worked on a movie with master filmmaker John Boorman of *Deliverance* fame, and when he found out my family came from County Cork, Ireland, he joked that the only good thing that ever came out of Cork was the road to Dublin — and so it is with the St. George hike. The road around Lake Wilcox is really the high point of this excursion.

77 Claremont

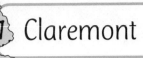

A couple of weeks ago, we drove the 401 east up to Westney Road in Ajax to the 7th Concession and the Durham Board Day Care Centre, which is really the front for the Claremont Conservation Area. And a sweeter hike you're never going to find. If the gates are open, go on in. If not, park and walk in. Stay to your left, down to Duffins Creek and then head north. You're going to see old trails and campsites everywhere. The area's been closed for years but they won't stop you. Just be careful and take a phone, and a camera, if you've got one, hikers. Stunning views of the river valley, dramatic erosions, upturned trees, nature and chaos, but in a nice way. And bonus, hikers, on the western side of the park there's a movie set of an old pioneer town from the late 1700s built for the television series "Little Men."

And be darned if Tracker Dave Bradstreet and I didn't find a dark, cool, inviting beaver pond with a waterfall, just north of the Forks of the Duffins. You have never seen two grown hiker men disrobe and hit the water so fast! Claremont is magical. Five stars. Mother Nature's cornucopia.

78 The Old Horseshoe: Don't Do It!

Not long ago I sneaked out of town for a hike by heading straight up Dixie Road from the 401, and as I headed straight into the Caledon Hills, I realized that Dixie Road had turned into Horseshoe Hill Road. And then I remembered that an old discontinued railroad line wound its way from the Caledon Trailway, switching back and forth up the steep walls of the Niagara Escarpment, eventually crossing under the Escarpment Sideroad perched at the top of the world a kilometre or two east of Caledon Town Centre and Highway 10.

I found the access one day walking the Caledon Trailway west of Heart Lake Road, but it was fenced up tighter than the Milton Hilton or the Don Jail. Definitely no hikers allowed from that entrance. So this time, I wanted to access it from either Heart Lake Road or the Escarpment Sideroad. But the snow was too deep and the fences too high to make the attempt that day. But while I was up top of the Escarpment Road, the view to the south and west was so astonishing from Toronto to Milton with Lake Ontario in the distance, I parked the car and hiked my way along the Escarpment Sideroad all the way down to Highway 10, where I could see the giant Devil's Pulpit and the Caledon ski trails high up in the mountains to the west.

Guerrilla Limits: Return to the Horseshoe

I've got to draw the line somewhere. Guerrilla hiking must be fun, adventurous, even a little dangerous, but when you find yourself crossing somebody's front lawn while they're having breakfast on their patio, it's time to pull in your guerrilla horns, hikers. And that's exactly what happened to me on the Old Horseshoe Railway line. If you climb to the top of the Escarpment Sideroad on the Horseshoe Hill Road, you'll notice on your left, the southwest corner, an elegant hilltop French chateau looking out over the Golden Horseshoe, all of the Megacity bowing at her feet, a truly majestic sight. Her grassy front-yard pasture is a half mile square surrounded with an endless four-bar wooden fence, while the cliffside looking south to the Lake is a multileveled terrace of sculpted greenery and statued patios leaving us agog at the scale of this vision.

We parked just before Kennedy Road where a winding snake-like gully crosses up from the south under the Escarpment Sideroad. We were so happy to find the grassy hump that once held the Old Horseshoe Railway bed, terribly overgrown with sumac and other garbage thickery, that we strapped on our backpacks and tumbled south down into the early morning hundred-year-old pathway. I say pathway optimistically, because there was little evidence underfoot, apart from the 4-foot ridge rising up to meet us out of the bottom of the canyon. Once we got into the groove, though we could see ahead where the trees parted, indicating the direction of the trail, which we gratefully followed over a garbage dump, along a pasture fence, into a deep, green forest tunnel, and out into the Chateau's backyard patio in full view of the "famille entière" sitting down to breakfast with a somewhat surprised look on their faces. We passed them so closely we could see the hollandaise sauce on top of their eggs benedict.

"Just passing through. Very sorry, folks. We're following the old railway line back into history. It'll never happen again," while hissing "Keep moving at all costs" to my Sherpa buddy Tracker Dave. Thank goodness we happened upon gentle, tolerant, break-fasters who just waved us on once they realized we meant no harm. In future I will be much more careful to not invade any private person's property. There is plenty of public land for exploration.

Please keep off private property, especially around the established hiking trails such as the Bruce, the Oak Ridges and the Ganaraska. The trail clubs have lobbied long and hard to get the landowners' permission to cross their land so trails can follow the more spectacular contours of the topography.

An all-too-painful example of hiking gone awry is the closure of the Upper Canada College grounds in Norval to hikers. For years the Bruce Trail passed through the grounds on the Credit Valley Footpath until just recently, when the trail was taken away from us because of vandalism. Now the Bruce must leave the river and follow a railway line and a well-used, noisy road in order to circumvent the campus. So don't go bugging landowners on your hikes, or we'll hear about it back at Hiker Headquarters, send out a posse, track you down and separate you from your Guerrilla Hiking License. I'm not recommending the Horseshoe Railway hike. My transgression at the Chateau was one too many and I've lost the taste.

Slightly Out of Town, Totally Out of Your Mind

Exceedingly Arduous Hikes

Algonquin Park: Maggie Lake and the Western Uplands Trail

Got a call from my old Urban Sherpa pal Beachman Gary. He missed his week on the Athabaska River because of the Air Canada strike, and decided instead to treat us both to the Western Uplands Trail hike in Algonquin Park. So no sooner did we finish our hosting duties at the United Way Walk-A-Thon than up the big highway we go to Huntsville — turn right and head east on Highway 60. And just before the Algonquin gates we stopped at Timber Trail cottages for a trout dinner, hiking preparations and a good night's sleep. They must have seen us coming because they charged us $150 for a dumpy little cabin with a black-and-white TV in the off season. Shame on you, Timber Trail. We'll not be by again.

Woke up at 6 am to the smell of Beachman's toast and coffee and the miserable sounds of rain, which turned to a cold drizzle, then stopped altogether by the time we got to the Western Uplands Trailhead just inside Algonquin Park. We knew we were about to spend 8 to 10 rigorous hours in the bush. Western Uplands Trail is rugged mountain terrain designed for backpackers in extremely good condition, used to hiking 15 to 25K a day.

The trail was wide and gracious, well marked with blue and white backpacker's signs every 50 feet or so. Then we hit the first hill (mountain, more like it), straight up into the forest. I was thankful to be carrying a 15-pound daypack instead of 45 pounds of backpack. The work of the trail maintenance crew was the best I've seen. All brush and fallen trees chain-sawed away from the trail, no overhang, bridges cut from pine and cedar logs in 4-foot lengths. Atop the mountains are rest stops, large smooth rocks where you can sit and rest without taking off the backpack, and the cleared trail was a foot-happy mix of loamy humus and pine needle.

About 90 minutes into the hike, the Western Uplands Trail turns off into a side trail of beautifully designed campsites surrounding crystal-clear, sandy-bottomed Maple Leaf Lake. That's the destination for most day-hikers. But keep to the main trail, towards Maggie Lake, unless you want a swim, because you give

up a lot of hard-earned high ground by heading down to the lake.

The section from Maple Leaf to Maggie Lake — two hours — is beyond the average hiker. Forget the Fitness Institute. Your pulse will be hitting 180 beats a minute trekking up these hills. You'll be energized if you're in top shape and you'll hit the golden groove. No mountain too high. The Body Factory open for business. Once past Maple Leaf, the trail roughs up and tapers off. It's rocky, less sure-footed, and dangerous. This is big-league hiking. Total silence. Only the birds, the breathing, the boots and the bears.

We eventually climb up into and around the other side of stunningly pristine Maggie Lake, find a waterfront campsite, light a fire to make some soup, hit the water for a cool-down, enjoy a lunch of oysters smoked with chocolate and oranges, find a comfy sunspot on pine needles, and snooze for an hour. On our way back, we recognize landmarks we've missed on the way up. One to look for is the world's most perfect Tom Thompson island sitting pretty in the middle of Steep Rise Lake. Hikers, you'll want to move there. It's heaven smiling on a little piece of earth. You're looking at eight solid hours in the bush. This ain't no waltz in the Black Forest.

It was mid-September when we hiked the Western Uplands Trail, and we passed loads of backpackers. Fall's the best time to go. Winter is impossible, spring too muddy, and the bugs make you a banquet in summer. And a tip of the hiker fedora to Gary Beechey for showing us the magic of Algonquin.

BEARS IN THE WOODS

My hiking friend Bushwacker Boris has alerted me that, in light of the rising frequency of conflicts between humans and grizzlies and black bears nationwide, the Ministry of Fish and Game is advising hikers, hunters and fishermen to take extra precaution and stay alert while in the field and on the trail. Outdoorsmen must wear noisy little bells on their clothing so as not to startle bears, and warn them in advance of our presence on their turf. We must carry pepper spray in case of an ursine encounter. It is a very good idea to know the difference between black bear and grizzly bear poop, as most bears find it comforting to poop in the dead centre of a human pathway.

Black bear poop is smaller and contains lots of berries and squirrel fur. Grizzly poop, on the other hand, has lots of bells in it and smells of pepper spray!

This little joke caused quite an uproar with hikers when I mentioned it on the radio but it also served to show how little we know about what to do when coming upon a large bear while hiking. So let's take the time here to dispel a few myths. First: female black bears with cubs are not as dangerous as males. Female black bears are notorious for simply abandoning their young in the face of adversity. Unfortunately, there's no way to tell the difference between a male and a female. Don't bother climbing a tree while trying to escape. Black bears are excellent climbers. Their scratch marks have been found in oak trees 60 feet above the ground. Black bears are also strong swimmers and don't truly hibernate. They're only winter "sleepers" and occasionally wake up and wander around, especially if provoked.

So what do you do if you're faced with a bear in the forest? According to bear expert Dr. Gino Ferri, prevention is the best advice. Let the animals know you're in the neighbourhood. Sing a song, make some noise if things are too quiet in the forest. Trust your instincts! When camping, hang your food bags in a tree away from the campsite, and never willingly feed the bears or you'll be sorry.

Surprising a black bear on the trail will agitate it, make it belligerent. The bear may roar, snort loudly, stomp its paws on the ground or pull a false charge, lunging at you then stopping. You should back away slowly and quietly, dumping any food you may have with you onto the trail in front of you as you retreat. A bear intent on predation will approach quietly on all fours in broad daylight and, without warning, rush its victim; the assault continues until the victim is killed, escapes, or the bear is forced to retreat. Whatever you do, do not play dead or the bruin will proceed to eat you.

Dr. Gino's advice to you is to fight back with everything available to you. Kick, scream, yell, bite, punch and strike with all your heart. Recorded cases indicate that bears are not fully aware of their ability to kill humans, and predatory attacks have been stopped when victims strike back, surprising the bear into retreat.

Thanks to Dr. Gino and *Bushwacker Magazine* June '99 issue for the timely bear advice. I would only like to add that when hiking in the forest and coming face to face with any large bear — *do not panic!* Just sit down immediately on the trail, put your head between your legs and kiss your ass goodbye. Talk about big, fat bums be gone, eh?

80 Kingsmere, Ottawa-Hull

I filed this report with CFRB on Canada Day, July 1, 1998. This is a special report from the nation's capital. Last Saturday I took a hike back into Canada's history and walked in the footsteps of William Lyon Mackenzie King and his little dog, Pat, through his magnificent estate, Kingsmere, 230 hectares of unspoiled beauty tucked away in Gatineau Park, just north of Ottawa.

We began our hike just behind King's farm, which is now the official residence of the Speaker of our House of Commons. A big redheaded woodpecker welcomed us to the waterfall trail leading downhill to the Stone Lookout over the falls — King's favourite spot. Then we took the Larrio Trail into the white pines until we came to the top of the Gatineau and a 180-degree panorama that I'll never forget, an endless patchwork of old Canadian farms and villages disappearing into the horizon. This hike made me proud to be a Canadian.

William Lyon Mackenzie King was born in Kitchener, my hometown, and he served as our prime minister for 22 years all the while improving both our country and his estate on the shores of Kingsmere Lake. Mackenzie King gave his life to his country, his expertise to his government, and when he died in 1950 he gave his magnificent estate to the Canadian people.

Getting to Kingsmere and the Larrio Trail is easy. Take Highway 5 north out of downtown Ottawa through Hull to Exit 12 — Old Chelsea and the Gatineau Parkway. Follow the signs to the King Estate about 20 minutes from Parliament Hill.

81 Temagami: Matabitchewan Trail

The Matabitchewan Trail in Temagami passes through an old-growth stand of glorious white pine some 25 kilometres due east of Highway 11, which just happens to be Yonge Street, 300 miles north of Toronto. This will be an all-day hike for me, into the Matabitchewan Lodge where my friend Dieter and his family live and run the lodge that was built in the '70s for the old Jimmy Cagney movie *Captains of the Clouds*.

This lumber road leaves Highway 11 about 45 miles north of North Bay, and 15 miles south of Temagami, at Gramp's Place Restaurant — Gas Bar — Bait and Tackle Shop. So stop into Gramp's for a drink before you start. Danny and Bonnie will show you the road and tell you about stopping by the dump to see the black bear family, sneaking up on the beaver colony in Rabbit Creek, where the blueberries and raspberries are hiding, and the best places to swim and fish for lake trout and pickerel.

Now, you don't have to hike all the way to Matabitchewan Lodge. Just 3 miles from Highway 11 on this old lumber road is Rabbit Creek Railway Crossing, where the Ontario Northlands

Train whistles through on its way to Hudson Bay — the creek's a perfect bug-free halfway point for a swim and a picnic. It's 3 miles in, plus lunch, plus 3 miles out, and hours of bliss. Wear your lowtop hikers, sunscreen and a hat, carry a small pair of binoculars for the deer, the moose and the hawks, and leave your car at Gramp's for safekeeping.

Temagami — you'll have a bear of a time!

82. Temagami, Northland Paradise

Hikers, you have to go to Temagami. It's northland paradise. Temagami is the home of, among other things, the White Bear Forest. Pristine virgin growth — extremely old — 10,000 years in the making, ever since the glacier moved back. Forest chock-a-block full of 350-year-old gigantic red pine, white pine, spruce, poplar and cedar. Thousands of acres of White Bear old-growth forest, and maintained, well-used trails take the hiker through areas that have never been logged or mined or disturbed in any way by the actions of man.

There's a 7K trail from downtown Temagami, and trail pioneer Doug Adams from Northland Paradise Lodge has fought from the beginning to keep this temple to Mother Nature free for hikers. There will be no shoreline development in the White Bear. Doug will guide you along a 3,000-year-old portage trail, following old Indian traplines into the centre of the White Bear, where the great Tree Spirit lives, and high atop Caribou Mountain to the fire lookout tower, which is the highest point on our Yonge Street. A favourite venue for painters and photographers along with hikers, Temagami is the non-consumptive eco-tourism capital of Ontario. Fishing excels, along with hiking. One of Doug Adam's hikers caught a 31-inch, 13-pound pickerel out by Flag Island then released it after taking the picture. Catch and release is regularly practised.

If you're looking for accommodation while hiking in Temagami, Rainy and Lillian Laperriere have a lovely big cottage and motorboat or canoe for rent by the day of week; call them at the Temagami Boat Livery, 705-569-3321. And if you're looking for the best damn guide west of the Ottawa Valley, give Doug Adams a call at Northland Paradise in downtown Temagami at 705-569-3791. Tell him you want to hike the trapline into the White Bear Forest, and you can also tell him that Hiker Mike says to stop talking so much on the trail and no smoking either.

83 Lake Temagami Hiking

One sunny summer morning, my old hiking pal Stormy Blake and I jumped into *Buckshot*, the steel-hulled boat, and made our way across a wide and glassy expanse of Lake Temagami up to the head of the southwest arm, to Four Canoe Portage and an old logging road that took us into the Temagami Island Nature Trail and the magnificent old-growth forest.

On the pine-needle-covered trail were plenty of signs of moose and bear. The trick is (a) not to step in any of it and (b) to talk up a storm so the big animals will hear you coming and think twice about having you over for dinner.

That's forest primeval, hikers. Three-hundred-year-old red and white pines towering straight up hundreds of feet into the blue. Stormy and I put our tree-hugging arms around the biggest red pine and we could just touch each other's fingers, which made it 13 feet around. Back on the trail, deep in the woods, old Rupert the Malamute refused to lead the hike and came and walked around behind me. There must have been danger ahead. So what did I do? Belted out a Broadway show tune as loud as I could!

We found the ancient native settlement at the south end of Temagami Island, and the mountain lookout surrounded by old-growth maple at the north end, and so can you, hikers. Phone Lady Evelyn Outfitters at 705-569-2595.

Temagami is a northland paradise specializing in non-consumptive eco-tourism and it's only a 4½-hour drive from downtown Toronto.

THE BAKA RAINFOREST PEOPLE

Cradled in the heart of the African rainforest lives one of the oldest and most fragile musical cultures of the Earth, and the music belongs to the Baka Forest people. The Baka use their music in magical ways during the hunting and harvesting times of year. The women go down into the river and, with their hands, set up a rhythm using the river as their drum. They fall into an animalistic canticle and pray to the spirit of the forest for game, gently slapping the water in time to the ancient rhythms. Most often the spirit of the forest smiles upon the Baka song and fills their river with fish, their trees with monkeys, their traps with deer, and their hearts with joy.

But all is not harmonious in nature. As with all indigenous people threatened by the oncoming hordes of civilization, these magical Baka Forest people are fighting to preserve their culture and their rain forest. You can help by dropping by your favourite record store and asking Sam to order the 1993 Rykodisc CD *Heart of the Forest — the Baka People*. A portion of the proceeds goes towards the preservation of their culture and everyone's precious rain forest. Once you hear the water drums of the Baka women in heart of the forest, it will haunt you forever.

Everglades Florida
Collier-Seminole State Park

Just 30 miles east of Naples, Florida, down the Tamiani Trail we now call Highway 41, is the Collier-Seminole State Park — a 6,000-acre mangrove preserve that is home to the endangered American crocodile, black bears, panthers, bobcats and, in its waters, what few manatees remain here on Earth. Boater Beware signs everywhere. The ecosystem's diversity consists of tidal creeks, mud flats, cypress swamps, and majestic pine savannah. And all of these wonders of nature can be accessed by way of a 6½-mile wilderness hiking trail through this jungle, and a 13-mile canoe trail along its canals and waterways.

After checking in with the visitor's centre, and filling out a hiker file absolving the State of Florida of any responsibility for our actions, Smokey gave us a trail map and an update of trail conditions, and into the park we went. We found the trail loop pretty wet, and since Smokey warned us about the gators and snakes, we decided to hike the 4-mile fire road instead. It took us through the Great Cypress Forest and across the pine savannah flatlands, which are cleared by fire every three years to encourage tree growth, so most of the surviving trees are marked by black char 5 or 6 feet up the tree bark. Lots of big animal tracks on the road, so unless you've done primitive hiking before, be prepared for wildlife and that feeling of imminent danger. Collier-Seminole Wildlife Refuge is careful not to disturb the Seminole tribe whose village lies at its centre.

The hike finished at noon, and we drove the 10 miles to Marco Island for a lunch of fresh, fat oysters and conch chowder at the Snook Inn, dining al fresco lulled by the soothing sounds of the Gulf of Mexico. Then off to hike the best-kept beach-hike secret on Marco Island — the Tiger Tail — 8 miles of virgin white sandbar cutting out into the gulf. We walked for hours on the hard-packed sand just above the waterline and watched a million hungry birds hunting for dinner.

85 Everglades City

Running down the southwest Florida coast, past the beaches of Fort Myers and the islands of Sanibel and Marcos, is the old Tamiani Trail, Highway 41.

Then, as if she can no longer abide the harsh sun and salt spray of the Gulf of Mexico, Tamiami charges headlong east into the Everglades, the old Alligator Alley, long and straight, through the Giant Cypress Reserve, pausing for only a moment at the gates of the Everglades National Park in Everglades City where the rainforest jungle says "howdy" to the gentle breezes of the Gulf. There are ten thousand islands here, a refuge teeming with endangered

wildlife: bottlenosed dolphin, the manatee in its shallow waters, and the Florida panther, dwelling in the hardwood hammocks (called hummocks in Canada) mounding up out of the flat swampy brown and gold of the ever-dangerous Glades.

There are no hiking trails as such in Everglades City — but just beyond, on Highway 41, is the Oasis Wildlife Center. It's like hiking in Holland, only wetter. The flat, grassy path just disappears into the swamp at times, making for squishy boots.

So head on up 41 to Monroe, Florida, and hike the Loop Road south following a gator canal with enough large and violent splashes to keep you on your toes. Park your car at the Everglades Sportsman's Club. They'll guard it for you unless a gator gets you. Then your car is theirs! Hike just 5 miles south of the club and a crystal spring and waterfall come right up to the road to meet you. So what you do is, shout real loud to scare off the gators, take off your hot and sweaty clothes, and ease your way in up to your neck to cool your jets, but keep your feet under you just in case you gotta jump out fast.

We'd been hiking all over the Glades for four arduous days but the whole campaign was completed with that swim. The mission was accomplished — the mandate satisfied. So now we could come home, tell the story and sing the song. We are stardust, hikers, we are golden. Now we've got to get back to the Summerhill Gardens. (Crosby, Stills, Kirby & Bradstreet)

86 West Indies: Grenada Hiking

The volcanic island of Grenada, complete with lush mountain rain forest and rich coral reef protecting pristine pink sandy beaches, lies at the bottom of the West Indies next to Barbados, Trinidad and Tobago. And it was to this island the Kirby family did go, armed only with our small backpacks, a change of underwear and a toothbrush on a voyage of discovery just before March Break '99.

It was an air-only voyage and, though we had an idea where we might stay, we hadn't locked in to accommodation. So imagine our surprise when we found the Grandview Inn high up in the jungle, looking out over the Caribbean, framed by a most stunning rainbow one moment, a torrential rainstorm the next, followed instantly by the sun's reappearance, causing the steam to rise from the jungle. Our mission was to hike the island for a week, and what better place to start than the 500-year-old harbour of St. George's, the capital of Grenada. So early on our first morning I accompanied the women to the market at the north end of the capitol, St. George's, and hiked my way back along the harbour, past the beautiful Grand Anse beach to the hotel district in the south by the airport — a distance of some 5 miles and a hike of an hour and a half.

The harbour in St. George's, Grenada, is just brim full of boats, fishermen, sailors, cruise ships, mail boats, freighters and a happy, bustling economy over which looms Fort George, where the Grenada–Cuban axis forces were defeated by Ronald Reagan's Yankees in the early '80s. The island architecture is hundreds of years old. Churches, post offices, public buildings, and a 150-year-old tunnel through the mountain connecting the inland market to the business district on the harbour. The entire city is surrounded by tall, green jungle mountains, the houses — built on concrete stilts to keep the termites at bay — marching their way right up to the jungle summits. And in the valley below, on the flat land, are the school and the playing fields. All of the government buildings and wharves are ancient and beautiful. Grenada is playing catch-up in the tourist business, and if you go there soon, you'll see the Caribbean as it used to be 50 years ago. But you'd better hurry, because the Ritz Carlton is coming.

Glass is a rarity in the houses in Grenada. It's not necessary as there are few bugs, and the weather is benevolent, so large shutters for closing against the rain and sun are enough. Grenada is cooled by the east-west trade winds. At noon hour it becomes almost unbearably hot and still, but then up comes a wind and it rains heavily for a few moments. And then the sun comes out again, steaming up the jungle, and so it goes through the day. There are 160 inches of rain in the jungle a year.

Grenada: Voyage to the Seven Sisters

We leave St. George's City with Mandoo, our hiker guide, travelling on a long, very well kept road, winding our way up into the forest higher and higher. The first thing you notice in the jungle valleys now below us are the giant immortalle trees, whose branches and leaves turn bright orange in the dry winter season. As we climb up past pretty pastel houses, fecund fields and animal-filled pastures, we begin to see the numerous reservoirs where the island's water is treated. Great jungle pools. You can drink the water here. Grenada is very user-friendly. You don't have to worry about venomous snakes, and you can hike and camp the mountains and the beaches wherever you like in Grenada.

Once inside the Grande Etang National Park, we take the turnoff for St. Margaret's River on the right and park the car. Mandoo changes his clothes and dons his high-top hiking boots, packs his cell phone and a papaya, and hacks us each a Moses stick with his machete, warning us that the going will be rough and muddy. Over the top we go. There are sections of this trail covered with nutmeg shells for traction — most hikers find it slippery but manageable.

We descend the mountain following the roar of the river for

45 minutes until we come to a large freshwater pool complete with 30-foot waterfall bull's-eyeing into its centre. Off with our clothes and into the pool we go. Once refreshed, Mandoo suggests we go for a little hike up the second section of trail to visit the Seven Sisters. I'm soaking wet in my bathing suit and I see no path but I say yes to everything. I follow Mandoo over to a vertical, muddy, rocky slope heading up beside the waterfall. For the next 20 minutes we climb like monkeys in our Speedos with our bare hands and feet until we reach the first sister, and for the next 15 minutes we swim and jump our way from pool to chute to water-fall until we are high atop the original pool staring down at our clothes next to the original pool. And over we go. Geronimo!

After a lunch of papaya, oranges and bananas, we re-don our hiking clothes and head back through the jungle to our car. Total time: 2½ hours roundtrip. Total calories burned: 2,000. On our way back we take the high-road loop. It spills us onto a grassy meadow with a nice easy road up the centre and flanked on both sides by recently planted Austrian pine with 6-inch feathers for branches. Everything grows big in the rain forest.

Slightly Out of Town

Mandoo's list of rain-forest gear:

1. A marine radio for emergencies;
2. a machete to cut your way through the jungle, fashion a Moses stick, or cut your way out from under a tree if it happens to fall on you;
3. a flashlight for night hiking, as there's no moon in the rain forest;
4. cell phone and a pager. Imperative to keep in touch with civilization; and
5. a first-aid kit.

The St. Margaret's River is the sweetest water I've ever tasted, and once the authorities in Grenada figure out how to harvest the majesty of this river, they'll have enough water for not only all its citizens but for the tourist industry as well. There's still time to hike Grenada before the rest of the world gets there. But hurry.

You can get a hold of Mandoo while you're in Grenada. He runs Grenada Tours and can be reached on the net through e-mail at Mandoo@caribsurf.com. He will take you on a kids and grandma hike around the crater Lake of the Grande Etange or down to see the Seven Sisters or, if you're an expert hiker, he'll take you high up into the clouds to the top of the island at Mount Qua Qua, 2,300 feet in the sky.

88 Grenada: Mount Qua Qua

Pulling into the parking lot of the Grande Etange National Rain-forest surrounding the volcano at the top of Grenada, we were met with a cacaphony of howls and screams coming from the jungle. Screaming is not uncommon here, as the revolutionary government took up refuge in the villa that now houses the Visitor's Centre during the Reagan raids in the island in 1983, but this time the shrill alarums were coming from the treetops where an entire family of Mona monkeys sat screaming for bananas — which our

trail guide Mandoo had in his backpack, for my kids to pass on.

And so began our ascent of Mount Qua Qua, a razorback-ridge hike to the top of Grenada. The trailhead was wide and paved with nutmeg shells crackling underfoot, but soon turned into a foot-wide mudslide climbing almost vertically through the rainy forest with Crater Lake falling away to one side and the town of St. Georges far off on the other. The trail is dangerous without a Moses walking stick or third leg. There are, however, tree-root footholds in the mud. High-top boots with a winter-tire grip are a must. Long, slim blades of razor grass line the trail. I grabbed some of it while sliding headlong down the trail and four weeks later I still had deep slices across my fingers which could have used a dozen stitches to be put right. So hiker, beware. Qua Qua is either a vertical climb, or a mud bath to the knees. But the workout is astonishing, and I counted my heartbeat at over 200 beats per second.

Among the benefits of rain-forest hiking high up in Grenada are a cooling wind and absolutely no bugs. The green and lush, broadleafed-jungle scenery will take your breath away. Lots of fern and pines, big old mahogany trees with Tarzan vines, and the biggest, fattest bamboo forests this side of Vietnam. After reaching the big rock at the top of Mount Qua Qua, you'll feel like Superman as you descend the 1,000 feet back into the oxygen.

There are many hikes from the Visitor's Centre at Grand Etang. So take your kids and grandmas, and they can do the Crater Lake and Lookout hikes, and feed the monkeys, who, I now find out, were not screaming for bananas when we arrived, but laughing in mocking derision when they found out I was about to climb Mount Qua Qua. So head to Grenada and hike Qua Qua. You'll come back refuelled with the joy of adventure.

FUTURE HIKES: CANADIAN HIMALAYAN EXPEDITIONS

My buddy Joe Pilaar from Canadian Himalayan Expeditions is again on his way to the Marka Valley in Ladakh up on the Tibetan Plateau for a two-week trek. This is the guy I went with to Everest Base Camp. We shared a tent at 18,000 feet. Joey wants you hikers to know that he's leading a team to the Nanga Parbat Base Camp in the Karakorum Range on the Silk Route Caravan Trail. Joey hikes year-round into the Himalaya by way of Annapurna Sanctuary and Everest Base Camp, and there's always room for experienced hikers. Small groups only — 12 to 16 — but you've got to be in great shape. If you're excited by the idea, call Joey at Canadian Himalayan Expeditions at 416-360-4300 and tell him Hiker Mike sent you. Joey and I will be heading back to the mighty Himalaya one day soon to three-peat the Base Camp Trek, but more on that later, possibly Volume 3, *Hike the Whole Damn World with Hiker Mike*.

FAT PEOPLE

On April 10, 1999, CFRB's Bill Carroll made a very brave statement on his Wall of Shame show, shouldered responsibility for his overweight poundage, and resolved to do something about it. Bill has opened the lid on the obesity problem — it's chronic, it's national, and we overweight people must acknowledge the fact or it will kill us before our time. I can speak to this national problem because there is a fat man inside of Hiker Mike and he's screaming to get out. Why do you think I hike so much?

We live in a wonderful country, a land full of opportunity and great restaurants. Just drive down any major street and look at the signs for buffets, smorgasbords, and all-you-can-eats for a very reasonable price. But what we save in money from the bargain groaning boards, our bodies pay for in our day-to-day unhealthy living. We're all overweight to a degree, fighting to return to those glory days of lean and mean, and we are losing the battle.

Fat people cost the health system $1.8 billion a year in treatment for hypertension, diabetes, heart attacks. People's waistlines are expanding the world over because of calorie-dense diets. Physical education is no longer mandatory at any of our schools. Kids are spending more time on the computer than on the playing fields. Then there's that hormone that flows from your fat cells to your brain telling you that you're hungry. Fat people have tried everything, and diets don't work. What's the answer? Doctors say that even if you lose only 10 percent, you start to reduce the risk of health problems. Most of us middle-aged guys are walking around with a 15-to-20-pound beer belly. Instead of taking pills for high blood pressure or injections for diabetes, wouldn't it be easier to incorporate a reduced diet and a little exercise?

Obesity is a medical epidemic. Now I've always maintained that if you can find it in your schedule to walk two hours a day, you can attack the smorgasbord with impunity and never be embarrassed about your weight at the beach again. Cellulite, on the other hand, is your own problem. So I'm going to say it once and once only, and very quietly. Okay? Are you ready, hikers? Say it with me: "Get up of your big fat bums and take a hike with Hiker Mike."

Kids' Hikes

TWO KIDS
ON A HIKE

Parents, if you're looking for something to do, some activities over the spring break, or single-parent quality time on weekends, hiking is the perfect activity. Fun with your kids, private time away from the house, and it's also a healthy thing to do. I know one of my kids has a bronchial condition but her lungs open up on the trail and she's in fine shape by the time we get home. Hiking's great exercise for the cardio and the vascular.

When I began hiking with my seven-year-old, Lucy, she had no problem with an hour hike for starters. The next week we did an hour and 40 minutes through some pretty rough terrain, and when we got back to the car she was quite surprised that the hike was over so soon. It doesn't take very long to get the kids up to speed, and before you know it, you'll be the one crying uncle. Kids, come on, give the old man a rest will you? Hiker Mike's feeling older by the day.

Make sure that the little darlings stay well back from cliff edges above the river valley, especially in the springtime, because the overhangs are quite precarious. There's no soil underneath, and if you stand on the edge, you're sure to go over. The wonderful thing about taking the kids is that, after you've hiked for an hour or so, you sit down, have a nice lunch, maybe a chicken salad, some muesli or some apples, and after a while the kids will go off and play. They can't sit still. In the meantime, you can lie in the sun and have a little nap and recharge your batteries for the trip home. Last Saturday after lunch the kids were playing McDonald's over by a big tree. Katy was the cook in the kitchen making the burgers, Lucy was the customer coming in to buy the burgers, and of course Maryanne, the oldest, was the manager, telling Katy how to make the burgers while Hiker Mike enjoyed a mid-afternoon spring snooze in a Carolinian sun pocket, high atop the Valley Rouge north of Old Finch.

Inner City: The Don and the Sauriol

The Sauriol Park and the Don River north of Pottery Road are two great kid's hikes. If you go to Lawrence and the Don Valley Parkway and park your car in the southeast quadrant under the Sauriol sign, you can hike south along the Don River pathway and high up along the sides of the Don Valley south to Eglinton and Sloane Drive. The whole hike takes you about an hour and a half and it's just perfect for kids.

There's also a great parking spot where Bayview Avenue meets the Pottery Road down in the Don Valley, and there's usually a flower guy named Murphy hanging around who'll watch your car for you. Make sure you find the path on the west side of the Don River just to the left of the railroad tracks, because that'll take you right into the forest. And you can follow the trail to the little bridge crossing the river a few kilometres to the north, putting you on the main road back downstream past the fish hatchery and the salmon-jumping cataracts. One hour, tops. The thing to do is to start out easy and walk as far as the kids want to walk. When they want to sit down and have a little rest, that's the time to break out some apples and some sandwiches. Then when you're rested, it will be the perfect little hike back to the car. Both trails have enough biodiversity to keep the kids interested: big hills they can scramble up and down and huge fallen trees hanging out over the river to swing on and play balance-beam.

The Beaches Boardwalk

Under the Boardwalk, down by the sea, hiking with the official photographer of CFRB, Gary Beechey, and our five kids. If you can imagine hiking on a wooden boardwalk, miles long, that's easy on your feet, with millions of kids and dogs and a Bahamian blue beach for swimming and sunbathing, then have I got a hike for you! It's the Beaches, Toronto's Riviera, the

Canadian Croissette, where everybody goes to breathe the air and get some exercise. Tennis courts, baseball diamonds, the Olympic swimming and diving pool, and refreshment stands, all the way from Neville Park to Ashbridges Bay.

How to get there? Leave your car at home and take the Queen Street trolley east to the Beaches, and walk south to the lake, or if you must drive, park at the foot of Coxwell in Ashbridges Bay. Bring your bathing suit, sunscreen, your picnic lunch, and a fishing pole because giant sabre-toothed salmon lurk just offshore. Have a nice swim.

Lost in Palgrave

Took the girls on an easy two-hour hike through Palgrave Forest last Saturday morning. Pulled into the gate just north of the village and headed west into the bottom of the forest. It's a good boot, but gentle, no big hills, so we covered the first half around the top of the forest to the other side where Finnerty Sideroad and Duffy's Lane meet. Sat down for lunch and ate a bunch of apples. Funny how the kids can't sit still for longer than two minutes. This time the midday entertainment included Maryanne and Katy climbing a steep sandy hill only to have a dead branch come off in Maryanne's hand, then Maryanne riding Katy to the bottom of the hill like a toboggan. Great fun! After lunch break, Hiker Mike got cocky and left the Red Trail that runs the circumference of the park, and struck out along a timber line with the three babes in tow. We got turned around down by a swamp, and because it was such a cloudy day with no sun to guide me, it wasn't long before we became hopelessly lost once again. And this was the day we had a hike deadline.

The babes had to be home for a birthday party at 4 pm, and now it was 3 pm and we were a good hour by car from home. A quiet panic started to set in. You know the one, "She's gonna kill me if I'm not home by four, life will not be worth living around the Hiker Homestead for a day or two." And it was right then that I spotted a shiny rooftop through the forest, and the promise of civilization — and a little help from a local human being who gave us directions back to our car and let me use his cell phone to call home and ward off the wrath of Mrs. Mike. And as we were leaving, we couldn't help but notice the CFRB van parked in his neighbour's driveway. "Why that's Taylor Parnaby's," he said. "Why don't you ring his buzzer and see if he's home?" And had we not been late for our appointment in Samarra, we'd have done just that. So what began as a two-hour hike ended up at almost four hours. I was so proud of the babes. The Palgrave adventure was their longest hike yet. We made it home a little late, a little the worse for wear, but no harm done.

Highway 50 north past Bolton, and Palgrave Village on the left over the second bridge. Look for the Kelley Tract sign and the gate into the forest.

Seaton Trail

Every Saturday morning the kids' hiking club explores a new trail, and this morning we're heading east on the 401 to Whites Road north a few miles and then right onto Forest Trail Road, which takes us down to the Seaton Trail on the Duffins Creek in Clarke's Hollow. The only way to access the Seaton Trail is to jump the stones across the river. The kids love to do that. From the last big rock to the far shore is a little log bridge and everybody made it except for Maryanne, who got herself a big fat soaker to start the hike, but after five minutes of splooshing along the trail, she forgot about it. The soaker went away.

The Duffins is a great river valley for kids' play, with cedar trees for hiding and Tarzan vines for swinging. The trail will take you high up into a hardwood forest before it descends into the Hollow, where you'll have to cross the bridge to the west side to continue your hike north to Whitevale.

The Seaton Trail running up the Duffins is just as spectacular as the Rouge River, one valley to the west, with one exception — no people traffic. We saw two other hikers all day. Blue and green

symbols and yellow rings on the trees mark the Seaton Trail. If you don't see these, you're on the wrong side of the river. We stopped just south of Whitevale and had a very nice lunch of Ritz crackers and apples and cold, crystal water right from the rapids of the Green River. It's important to let the kids rest when they want to. Use the time for jokes or tall tales and get them into the art of storytelling, and before you know it everybody will be laughing and rested and ready to go again.

Our family is getting used to the idea of all-day walks and we're starting very slowly with two-hour hikes every Saturday morning. Then we'll work our way up to Algonquin Park, where we'll pitch a tent at the trailhead and go for all-day hikes for 8 to 10 hours, then come back to the tent, cook our food over an open fire and watch the stars and listen to the wolves howl and just have great family fun, before it's too late.

Tried-and-True
Hall of Fame

I've got a true story to tell you. I wouldn't be hiking the trails today without my hiking boots and I'll tell you why. I was hiking the western ridge of the Boyd Conservation Area up in Wood-bridge when I ran out of path at the top of the ridge. Erosion had washed out the high trail, and now there was nowhere to go but straight down into the rocky river valley some hundred-odd feet below. The vertical looked pretty steep — no path, just loose earth and the occasional tree, possibly to help me down by slowing my descent. So I planned my route and jumped over the side, and it wasn't long before my feet were working quicker than my head. Pretty soon I was running full out, heading for the rocks below me, so to slow my speed I leaned out to grab a passing tree, and the tree broke off in my hand, and the dust from the disinte-grating tree got into my eyes. So now I'm flying blind. By all rights, I should have crashed and burned and broken every bone in my body. I was totally out of control. So imagine my surprise when I found myself standing upright at the bottom of the ravine with what's left of the tree in my hand. I had just gotten away with murder. My own. So give credit where credit's due, right? And that's just what I did. I bent right over, put my hands on my knees and, blinking away the dusty tears, said, "Thank you" to my hiking boots.

I've been a Merrell Boot guy for over 10 years. Wore them twice to Base Camp. Great fit, no break-in time. Hiking boots are the heart of your hiking gear. Choose wisely. And if you need a lit-tle help getting a good pair to fit, call my boot guy Arnold Tsu at Sporting Life on Yonge Street, 416-485-1611. Arnold is fastidious in the fitting department. Take advantage.

I had the opportunity to work for 3 to 4 hours the other day in the snow, in those same boots. Hard work it was, carrying heavy equipment knee-deep in snow, and the labour was continuous and arduous. We got very hot and sweaty, waterlogged from the knees down. My boots and SmartWool socks were soaked but the Smart-Wool kept trying to wick away the moisture from my hopelessly wet feet. And somehow there was warmth being produced. Although my feet were soaking wet, they were nice and toasty warm on the ride home. The combination of good hiking boots and SmartWool socks will keep you warm under the worst conditions.

#1 LoweAlpine Vision 40 Backpack

Hikers, my backpack holds my life in its folds. It's my office, my wardrobe, my library, and my kitchen on the trail. If you've ever heard me play What's in My Backpack? with Donabie on CFRB, you know how rugged, waterproof, versatile and comfortable my backpack must be. And so it was with great pleasure that I accepted a LoweAlpine Vision 40 backpack from Michael Maysell at Daymen Distributors.

Michael suggested I try the Vision 40 expandable backpack made by that great mountain-gear company from Colorado,

LoweAlpine. Up to now I have been a big fan of the Mountain Equipment Co-Op daypack — one big compartment with a zippered pocket for wallet and keys, et cetera. But I am a tall man, and the LoweAlpine Vision 40 not only boasts a long thin line, but also the back padding connects with, and runs down, the muscles on either side of your backbone, leaving an air groove so your spine can breath free. And when you do up the chest and waist buckles, the Vision 40 fits to your body like a comfy old sweater. Three zippers in the top flap, for radio, keys, wallet and your novel. A long pocket zips down the front of the pack for maps and a cell phone, and deep water-bottle pockets on the bottom side of the Vision 40 makes it easy to reach down and back for a quick drink in mid-stride.

Bonus. The Vision 40 is expandable — loosen the straps on the side of the pack and it accordions outward to form a large backpack able to carry 25 to 30 lbs. Tighten the straps and you're back to a daypack for camera, socks, and your book and water. The only downside for me is I didn't agree with the choice of colour, but that's personal. You got your lime green, Halloween orange, bright gold or cobalt blue. The upside is, the big wildlife will see you coming and run for their lives! It's the best damned backpack that anybody's ever given me. So congrats to Michael Maysell and Daymen Distributing for the LoweAlpine Vision 40 — the snuggle bunny of backpacks.

#2 Salomon Boots

I was asked to give a talk on the beauties of the Bruce Trail at Novak's Hiking Store on King Street in London, Ontario, for Hike Ontario Week, in association with Angie Brooks of Boston Mills Press. We discussed a half a dozen different Bruce Trail hikes where Bruce meets up with the 401, providing easy access for hikers coming from the London area. We had a great hour. We played What's in My Backpack? and read the Hiker Mike radio reports out loud, and gave away David Bradstreet CDs.

Owner Paul Kaplan noticed that I was wearing my Salomon summer hiking boots and asked me if I'd be interested in trying out a pair of extreme winter hiking boots. I said "absolutely," as I was a big Salomon boot fan, and thought nothing more of it until the FedEx guy delivered a couple of beautiful new Salomons to my door. These soft but rugged waterproof boots took me 10K to the top of Scrabble Mountain on the Ganaraska Wilderness Trail the first time I put them on. No callouses, no corns, no blisters, just 20K roundtrip of beautiful hiking through very rough bush. That's just one of the joys of Salomon boots — no break-in time. Try them on, lace them up and hit the bush, hikers. So, many thanks to Paul Kaplan at Novak's Hiking Store on King Street in London, for my new boots.

Hikers, if you're down London way, drop in, say hi to Paul and Mike and check out the store. Everything you need to get you through four seasons of rigorous hiking, plus an extensive library of hiking books and maps on the second floor.

I'VE GOT YOU NEXT TO MY SKIN

My pal over at Canadian Himalayan Expeditions, Joe Pilaar, just got back from Morocco and the Atlas Mountains, where he put together a hike from Marrakesh to Mount Toubkal (third-highest mountain in Africa). Looks just like the Tibetan Plateau, says Joe, so much so that Martin Scorsese shot his Himalayan picture, *Kundun*, there. Even in quasi-equatorial Morocco, it can get damned cold in the mountains.

So, with the heavy weather starting to set in, I want to say a few words about the proper clothing for the next six months. Now, cold weather hiking is great fun if you're dressed properly, so give me the four layers of clothing, starting with what goes next to your skin.

1. Cotton longjohns.
2. Fleece synthetic or wool turtleneck sweater.
3. Wind and waterproof Gore-Tex shell.
4. Down parka to pull on over the bum when the long trek is over, or just lounging over a smart lunch of oysters, chocolate and oranges.

CHAPTER 15

In Closing

YES.   MAYBE.   NO.

A Note from Tracker Dave Bradstreet

You know, hikers, I've had the good fortune to hike the world from the Himalayas to the Rockies, and it seems to me that we are very fortunate to have so many world-class hikes right here in and around Toronto — wonderful facilities, most of which are

provided by the Metro Conservation Authority. Places such as Kortright Conservation Area, the Rouge Valley, Palgrave Forest, and the Humber Arboretum all offer hikes for various skill levels and adventures.

Thanks to the MCA for doing such a good job of watching out for the welfare of the parklands, riverbanks and trails, in some cases taking the very prudent position of leaving them alone. And as more people discover the fitness benefit of hiking, our trails will become the place to be on a beautiful weekend morning, or in the evening after a hard day's work. Hiking doesn't cost very much — a good pair of shoes, a hat, a coat is really all you need, as long as you dress for the weather. So in these days of cutbacks and minimal funding by government, it is a wonder that these conservation areas can survive at all with no budgets for maintenance or promotion and advertising.

Perhaps we hikers need to entice our local vocal politicians to come out with us and have a good look at how truly beautiful these conservation areas are; then we would have more supportive voices at Queen's Park and Metro Hall to spread the word and perhaps direct a few more bucks into MCA promotion budget.

You know, it took dedicated people like Tommy Thompson and ex- Metro Conservation Chairman Bill Granger to create these beautiful trails. The trails are like anything else: neglect them and they wither — love them and they flourish and grow. So come on, Mayor Mel and Premier Mike. Get off your big fat surplus and take a hike with Hiker Mike in our Metro Conservation Areas!

Hike Ontario Day

The first Sunday of October is Hike Ontario Day. Over 300 trail clubs, youth groups, conservation areas, coureurs de bois and Urban Sherpas participated in Hike Ontario Day by organizing a hike. Hike Ontario Day raises awareness and support for hiking trails in Ontario and introduces new hikers to the spirit, mind and body benefits of hiking: a perfect time for all you wannabe hikers out there to join up with Hike Ontario by becoming a member and taking a hike leadership course. All you have to do is call my old pal Harold Sellers at Hike Ontario 416-426-7362 and tell him Hiker Mike sent you.

Reminiscences of a Twelve-Year-Old

Tracker Dave and Hiker Mike and the rest of the gang of the Urban Sherpas, we're all of an age, but we all know what it feels like to be 12 years old. Remember when you were just old enough to get out of the house, get permission to spring free, go away and explore for an afternoon? You grab hold of your bike, get some bait, some dew worms, a Popeil Pocket Fisherman, make a couple of peanut-butter sandwiches, and hit the country roads. Bike out of town to the river where you find the trail, ditch your bike in the bush, and follow the trail deep into the forest upriver where you set up camp next to the fishing hole, go for a swim and toast your PB & Js over an open fire, and head for home before it gets too dark and you become hopelessly lost and you have to call your dad from the gas station to come and get you. Humiliating!

I was a lucky kid. I got to go to camp when I was five years old, because my mom was a Cub Scout leader and she made

sure I was included with the bigger kids' activities. So every year at camp I got a new badge — all Indian names — Tenderfoot first year, then Brave, Warrior, Little Chief, Big Chief, CIT, then Counsellor. And every year the overnight camping trips got longer, so I finally got to spend a month hiking and canoeing in the wilderness. Actually my 18th summer on Earth was spent entirely at camp — waterfront director, lifeguard, cookhouse boy for two whole months. I was made for the job. Half the summer the camp was full of boys and the other half were girl campers with hot counsellor babes. Just try to imagine the fun I had! Every night at campfire we'd close proceedings with that wonderful old chestnut, "When the one Great Scorer comes to mark against your name, it matters not if you win or lose, it's how you play the game."

It was a wonderful time of self-discovery and I still get excited just thinking about it. The fun I had racing through the bush when I was 12 years old still lives within me when I'm hiking the forest trails today almost half a century later. How old is that Hiker Mike, you say to yourself? Now you know, hikers. The answer is 12 years old. Always was and always will be. Show me a hiking trail long enough and you'll never see me again.

Centenary Hiking

We should plan on a birthday hike to celebrate our hundredth year on Earth. Most experts say spend two hours of walking a day and you'll live to be a hundred. So it's incumbent on us to take the long view and be prepared. What's your favourite hike? Where on Earth would you like to spend your hundredth birthday? Tramping the Sea-to-Sea Trail in Britain or slogging through the rain forests of New Zealand? This is not outrageous speculation on my part, hikers. We will be living one hell of a lot longer than we ever dreamed, so we'd better be in good and flexible condition to enjoy our Golden Years. It's a simple proposition: Our mandate is to keep our spirit strong and positive, our mind keen and sharp and full of good humour, and our body in excellent physical condition, until such time as science finds the key to turning off the age gene. Then we get to cruise on into the next millennium along-side our kids and grandkids.

You see hikers, I was born just nine months ahead of the rest of you Boomers. All your soldier and sailor fathers came back when war ended in 1945, but my dad snuck back to get married in November 1944. So I got to be born on September 1, 1945, just a little ahead of the Great Horde, so I've always felt the Boomer's wishes and desires strongly. And among the many qualities with which the Boom Generation has been endowed is the desire to live forever. If this can be accomplished by science, physical activity, good pharmaceuticals, and sheer desire, the Boomer's will be done. Bank on it! So, hikers, get ready to live well into the excitement that is our future and don't forget to call old Hiker Mike on your hundredth birthday. If I can stand up and move forward, one foot then the next, I'll go hiking with you. Thank you if you've read this far. That's all there is. There isn't any more.

Thank Yous

Many people helped in the creation of this book. Hike Ontario past president Peter Heinz was very encouraging when I began the hiking report some years ago.

Thanks to my wife, Libby, who assisted me in every way during the production of this book, without whose lightning-quick typing fingers, the calming hand on my shoulder, and organized mind, the work would never have been completed.

It was John Donabie, my weekend host at CFRB, who suggested that I call in "live from the trail," and program directors Bob Mackowycz and Steve Kowch, who programmed the reports into the Weekend Morning Show. Thank you, and thanks to big boss Gary Slaight, who actually pays me for doing what I love — talking and hiking.

Thank you to my hiking buddies, the Urban Sherpas: Captain Karl Pruner, television star and global hiker; Beachman Gary Beechey; Tracker David Bradstreet, my bestest and oldest pal; Stormy Blake Stormes, for showing me the trail up Temagami way; actress Linda Sorenson; Dudley the Dragon and his maker,

Jiminy Rankin; and Shakespearean street actor John Evans. Thank you Lorne and Dorie Preston from Port Union, who took me on my first Megacity Hike up Highland Creek. Thank you Professor Ken Bartlett from Vic, who helped me find my Renaissance Man.

Thanks to the Astrocat himself, Marcos Sorenson, creative director for Ask Jeeves.com, who supplied art for the Hiker Mike cover and the hiker icons, and to Lisa Rotenberg for creating the Secret Map of All Hikes. Thank you generous Uncle Doug Paulson, Canada's number-one voice guy, for sharing his Vault Sound Studios in Toronto, and CFRB production gurus Bob Lehman and Dave LeBlanc, who helped me put the Hiker Mike Reports together. Thank you super agent Lynn Kinney for putting this book deal together, and God bless Angie Brooks from Boston Mills Press, who talked John Denison and Noel Hudson into publishing this book. And the award for patience and good grace must go to my editor, Kathleen Fraser, whose job it was to make good sense out of my random chaos.

And most of all I'd like to thank my mother, Mary Ann Kirby, whose candid words are with me still: "Mike, you sure talk a good game. Now let's see if you can make a living."

WE'VE GOT NUMBERS

Hike Ontario. 416-426-7362
The Avon Trail, London 519-271-8730
Bruce Trail Association 1-800-665-4453
Elgin Hiking Trail Club, Port Stanley 519-433-7698
Ganaraska Trail Association . . . . 905-885-4430.
Grand Valley Trails Association, Orangeville. 519-745-5252
Guelph Hiking Trail Club 519-822-3672
Humber Valley Heritage Trail Association, Bolton. 905-857-3743
Lynn Valley Trail, Simcoe/Port Dover. 519-428-3292
Maitland Trail Association, Goderich 519-524-6988
Menesetung Bridge Association. 519-524-6988
Oak Ridges Trail Association, ... 905-852-7128
Rideau Trail Association, Ottawa/Kingston 613-545-0823
Sudbury Hiking Club. 705-523-5480
Thames Valley Trail Association, London 519-645-2845
Voyageur Trail Association, Sault St. Marie 705-253-4470
Waterfront Trail. 416-314-9490
Wellesley Trails Association, Kitchener 519-656-2670
Oxford Trail Association 519-475-4630
Lost River Walks 416-781-7663
Durham Outdoors Club, ... 905-436-0633
Sweet Josie Trails 613-584-2468
4-Day Evening Walks 905-383-6319
Elora Cataract Trailway 519-843-3650
Camping Info, Provincial Parks for Ontario 1-800-ONTARIO
TTC Information 416-393-4636
Metro Conservation Authority 416-661-6600
Albion Hills Campground. 905-880-4855
Indian Line Campground. 905-678-1233
Winnebago Rental 1-800-616-CAMP
CFRB access line to leave a message for Hiker Mike. 416-872-1010

email me: hikermike@hikermike.com